# COOKING WITH A WOK

# Cooking with a

WOK

**Bridget Jones**

WITHDRAWN

**Hamlyn**

London · New York · Sydney · Toronto

Photography by James Jackson
Line drawings by Joyce Tuhill

The author and publishers would like to
thank Salton Ltd. for the loan of an
electric wok for photography and
recipe testing.

First published in 1984 by
The Hamlyn Publishing Group Limited
London · New York · Sydney · Toronto
Astronaut House, Feltham, Middlesex, England
© Copyright The Hamlyn Publishing Group Limited 1984

ISBN 0 600 32388 9

Phototypeset in Monophoto Apollo by
Servis Filmsetting Limited, Manchester, England
Printed in Italy

# Contents

# Useful Facts and Figures

## Notes on metrication

In this book quantities are given in metric and Imperial measures. Exact conversion from Imperial to metric measures does not usually give very convenient working quantities and so the metric measures have been rounded off into units of 25 grams. The table below shows the recommended equivalents.

| Ounces | Approx g to nearest whole figure | Recommended conversion to nearest unit of 25 |
|---|---|---|
| 1 | 28 | 25 |
| 2 | 57 | 50 |
| 3 | 85 | 75 |
| 4 | 113 | 100 |
| 5 | 142 | 150 |
| 6 | 170 | 175 |
| 7 | 198 | 200 |
| 8 | 227 | 225 |
| 9 | 255 | 250 |
| 10 | 283 | 275 |
| 11 | 312 | 300 |
| 12 | 340 | 350 |
| 13 | 368 | 375 |
| 14 | 396 | 400 |
| 15 | 425 | 425 |
| 16 (1 lb) | 454 | 450 |
| 17 | 482 | 475 |
| 18 | 510 | 500 |
| 19 | 539 | 550 |
| 20 ($1\frac{1}{4}$ lb) | 567 | 575 |

*Note:* When converting quantities over 20 oz first add the appropriate figures in the centre column, then adjust to the nearest unit of 25. As a general guide, 1 kg (1000 g) equals 2.2 lb or about 2 lb 3 oz. This method of conversion gives good results in nearly all cases, although in certain pastry and cake recipes a more accurate conversion is necessary to produce a balanced recipe.

**Liquid measures** The millilitre has been used in this book and the following table gives a few examples.

| Imperial | Approx ml to nearest whole figure | Recommended ml |
|---|---|---|
| $\frac{1}{4}$ pint | 142 | 150 ml |
| $\frac{1}{2}$ pint | 283 | 300 ml |
| $\frac{3}{4}$ pint | 425 | 450 ml |
| 1 pint | 567 | 600 ml |
| $1\frac{1}{2}$ pints | 851 | 900 ml |
| $1\frac{3}{4}$ pints | 992 | 1000 ml (1 litre) |

**Spoon measures** All spoon measures given in this book are level unless otherwise stated.

**Can sizes** At present, cans are marked with the exact (usually to the nearest whole number) metric equivalent of the Imperial weight of the contents, so we have followed this practice when giving can sizes.

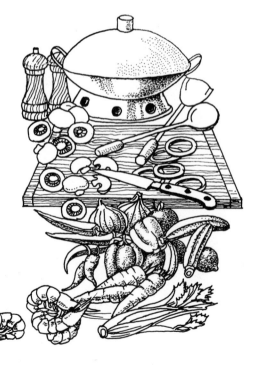

## Oven temperatures

The table below gives recommended equivalents.

|  | °C | °F | Gas Mark |
|---|---|---|---|
| Very cool | 110 | 225 | $\frac{1}{4}$ |
|  | 120 | 250 | $\frac{1}{2}$ |
| Cool | 140 | 275 | 1 |
|  | 150 | 300 | 2 |
| Moderate | 160 | 325 | 3 |
|  | 180 | 350 | 4 |
| Moderately hot | 190 | 375 | 5 |
|  | 200 | 400 | 6 |
| Hot | 220 | 425 | 7 |
|  | 230 | 450 | 8 |
| Very hot | 240 | 475 | 9 |

## Notes for American and Australian users

In America the 8-fl oz measuring cup is used. In Australia metric measures are now used in conjunction with the standard 250-ml measuring cup. The Imperial pint, used in Britain and Australia, is 20 fl oz, while the American pint is 16 fl oz. It is important to remember that the Australian tablespoon differs from both the British and American tablespoons; the table below gives a comparison. The British standard tablespoon, which has been used throughout this book, holds 17.7 ml, the American 14.2 ml, and the Australian 20 ml. A teaspoon holds approximately 5 ml in all three countries.

| British | American | Australian |
|---|---|---|
| 1 teaspoon | 1 teaspoon | 1 teaspoon |
| 1 tablespoon | 1 tablespoon | 1 tablespoon |
| 2 tablespoons | 3 tablespoons | 2 tablespoons |
| $3\frac{1}{2}$ tablespoons | 4 tablespoons | 3 tablespoons |
| 4 tablespoons | 5 tablespoons | $3\frac{1}{2}$ tablespoons |

An Imperial/American guide to solid and liquid measures

### Solid measures

| Imperial | American |
|---|---|
| 1 lb butter or margarine | 2 cups |
| 1 lb flour | 4 cups |
| 1 lb granulated or caster sugar | 2 cups |
| 1 lb icing sugar | 3 cups |
| 8 oz rice | 1 cup |

### Liquid measures

| Imperial | American |
|---|---|
| $\frac{1}{4}$ pint liquid | $\frac{2}{3}$ cup liquid |
| $\frac{1}{2}$ pint | $1\frac{1}{4}$ cups |
| $\frac{3}{4}$ pint | 2 cups |
| 1 pint | $2\frac{1}{2}$ cups |
| $1\frac{1}{2}$ pints | $3\frac{3}{4}$ cups |
| 2 pints | 5 cups ($2\frac{1}{2}$ pints) |

NOTE: WHEN MAKING ANY OF THE RECIPES IN THIS BOOK, ONLY FOLLOW ONE SET OF MEASURES AS THEY ARE NOT INTERCHANGEABLE.

# Foreword

*Wok cooking is fun cooking and it can be extremely practical too. I first bought my wok for cooking Chinese meals – mainly stir-fries and braises – but later discovered that it is ideal for all sorts of cooking: foods can be casseroled or steamed in the wok and they don't have to be oriental in flavour. Whenever I cook in my wok I take it to the table so that the food is served piping hot, and not only is it great fun eating in this way but it saves on the washing up too.*

*When testing these recipes I used three types of wok – a traditional carbon steel one, a non-stick one and an electric wok – so you can be sure that the dishes will be successful whatever sort of wok you own. Apart from all the fun of cooking in a wok, you are sure to be pleased with the practical aspects of your wok's performance as a cooking pan because it really is enormously useful.*

*While I was having fun testing these recipes, Neill, my husband, assured me that he enjoyed eating them, but at the same time he did not escape the bustle in the kitchen and on many occasions he rescued me from beneath an ever-increasing pile of washing up. Sometimes I think he deserves a medal for the support he gives! For deciphering my hurried, and not so neat, typing, thanks are also due to Frances Dixon who edited this book.*

*Most important of all, I hope that you will enjoy 'wokery', as I like to call it, and find the ideas throughout these chapters both inspiring and delicious.*

*Bridget Jones*

**Right** *clockwise, from the top:* stainless steel wok, non-stick coated wok, electric wok, carbon steel wok and a selection of useful accessories
**Overleaf** Mixed Soup Pot (page 24)
**Page 12** *top:* Chicken and Sweet Corn Soup (page 19); *bottom:* Spinach and Bean Curd Soup (page 23)

# Introduction

The wok is a thin, curved metal pan traditionally used for Chinese cooking. In other Asian countries similar cooking vessels, going by different names, are also used. In India, for example, such a pan would be called a *karahi*, in Burma it would be known as a *dar-o* and in Indonesia, Malaysia and Singapore it would go by the name of *kuali* or *wajan*. To think of a wok simply as a centuries-old frying pan is quite unfair because it is infinitely more versatile and far better designed than the average frying pan or skillet. Originally beaten out of tempered steel to heat up quickly, and curved to fit snugly over the flames of a Chinese brazier, the wok can be used for frying and stir-frying, braising and steaming; even a whole chicken or duck can be cooked in the wok!

In spite of these ancient origins the scope of this cooking utensil can be extended well beyond ethnic cooking, and the wok can be used for virtually all the cooking techniques (except oven cooking) used in a modern Western kitchen. Even though carbon or tempered steel woks are the ones most widely sold, non-stick coated, stainless steel and even electric types are now available. Except for the electric woks, which of course plug into the electricity supply, all the others can be used on either gas or electricity and they can also be utilised for table-top cooking. All in all, wok cooking is fun cooking; the adaptability of this vessel makes it most suitable for light-hearted food preparation. This is not the pan for the cook who wants to spend hours slaving over a liaison of eggs and cream; it is for the carefree cook.

## Types of wok available

The traditional and most common type of wok is that made from carbon or tempered steel. In addition, stainless steel woks and those with a non-stick coating are also available. Plug-in electric ones are made of carbon steel or they can be non-stick. Generally, the wok is completely curved, but there are some which have slightly flattened bases and these are particularly useful for electric hobs. Away from the Chinese supermarkets, ethnic shops and specialist cook shops, most woks are sold in kit form, complete with a stand, lid, steaming rack and a variety of small accessories. It is important to make sure that your wok has a good lid – well domed and well fitting, and *not* made of carbon or tempered steel. Look at the type of handles on the wok; some have a pair of metal handles – these will become very hot during cooking – while others have a pair of handles with wooden grips or a single wooden handle, both of which are quite practical. Before you buy a wok think about how often you are going to use it and what cooking techniques you are going to use it for, then look around and decide which type you would prefer. The following notes may be of some help when you are trying to decide, but also read through the notes on accessories before you part with your cash!

**Carbon steel or tempered steel wok** This is the traditional type of wok. Made of thin metal, a wok like this heats up very quickly and it is very responsive to an increase or decrease in heat. However, without care, this type of wok rusts easily – it needs to be kept oiled and free from damp. Ideally, a carbon steel wok should be used fairly frequently, in which case it is the best type to buy. After extensive use the steel builds up an excellent cooking surface – blackened, and not one which sticks easily. Make sure the lid is either of stainless steel or aluminium; a carbon steel lid presents a permanent rust problem and it can be a great nuisance!

So, if you plan to use your wok all the time, buy one of this type and make a real effort to give it hard use for the first few weeks to build up the cooking surface. But do be honest with yourself and, if you are only going to rummage in the cupboard for your wok on a biennial basis, then go for one of the other types.

*Care and storage* New carbon steel woks have a wax coating which has to be removed by scouring the wok in hot soapy water. The wok should be rinsed and thoroughly dried, then seasoned. To do this heat the wok and pour in a little oil, then rub it around the pan with a pad of absorbent kitchen paper. Heat the wok until it is smoking hot, wipe it again and repeat once more. Wipe the outside of the wok with oil too.

After cooking with fat, there is no need to wash the wok – it should be washed as rarely as possible – simply wipe it out with plenty of absorbent kitchen paper and use salt as a scouring agent, with a little fresh oil to clean the surface. If you have prepared a saucy dish or one which has stuck slightly, then wash the wok in soapy water and re-season it. This type of wok is best kept hanging in a dry, well-ventilated place.

**Stainless steel wok** This does not have the same rust problems as a carbon steel wok but it does not reach as high a temperature and it is not as responsive to temperature changes. It is also more prone to damage from scratching than the carbon steel type. However, some stainless steel woks have a slightly flattened base which makes them useful for electric rings and eliminates the necessity for a stand.

*Care and storage* Wash a stainless steel wok in hot soapy water, keeping the cooking surface lightly oiled for best cooking results. A special stainless steel cleaner can be used on the wok and after use the wok can be stored in a cupboard with no fear of rusting.

**Non-stick coated wok** Again, this type of wok does not rust and most have a slightly flattened base. They do not heat up as quickly as the carbon steel woks and they are not quite as responsive to heat changes, but they do have their advantages in that they are very easy to clean and, depending on the quality of the coating, they do not stick at all. Remember not to use metal utensils on non-stick surfaces. This type of wok is only as good as the coating on the cooking surface.

*Care and storage* Always follow the manufacturer's instructions for the care of non-stick utensils. This usually involves washing the wok in hot soapy water; it should never be scoured during cleaning.

**Electric wok** I was most impressed with the electric wok which I tested – it was an attractive, efficient appliance. The notes on the non-stick wok also apply to an electric wok, which has a non-stick coating. An electric wok is, in fact, an independent worktop cooker which is ideal for the bedsit cook with no other cooking facilities. Not only can complete meals be cooked in the wok, but they can also be served from it. I even took mine out into the garden on an extension lead to add a new dimension to barbecued food!

Look for an appliance with a detachable lead (like an electric kettle) and check the instructions to see whether the wok can be immersed in water for cleaning.

*Care and storage* Always follow the manufacturer's instructions for cleaning electrical appliances. This type of wok is best kept out on the work top in the kitchen.

## Accessories

Most woks come complete with a stand to place over the cooker hob. With sloping sides, these metal stands can be used to hold the wok near to the heat source, as required in the case of an electric ring, or it can be turned over to keep the wok above a gas flame. These stands can also be purchased separately.

Second only in importance to the stand is the lid. This is the other basic accessory needed for braising and steaming in the wok. Make sure that the lid fits well and that it has a wooden knob or one which will not become too hot when in use. A steaming rack is also important for cooking in the wok and it is usually included in wok kits; if not, one can be bought separately or a round, suitably sized cake rack can be used instead.

A variety of small accessories, such as ladles and spoons for tossing, turning, stirring and draining foods, is also available. These are not essential – if you have a reasonably well-equipped kitchen then you do not need them – but they do add to the fun of cooking in your wok.

Bamboo steamers are very useful because they can be rested over the wok and several layers can be stacked one on top of another, to cook and reheat a selection of dishes at the same time. If you are going to buy a set, choose those with a reasonably large diameter so that you can fit large dishes inside.

In addition, chopsticks and small bowls are useful if you are planning to prepare Chinese food. These are sometimes included in wok kits.

## Cooking techniques

Wok cooking is usually quite fast, so prepare all the ingredients in advance and you won't have any problems. If·you follow the recipe instructions fairly closely you will find that all the foods are prepared in the order which is necessary for successful cooking. Once you've used your wok for a while you will become accustomed to the speed with which it heats up and you will know how long in advance to turn on the heat.

**Stir-frying** This is the method most commonly associated with wok cooking and a traditional type of wok is by far the best appliance for this rapid food frying. The hot deep sides of the wok provide a large surface area and plenty of depth to sear and toss the food without throwing it out of the pan. It is most important to have all the ingredients ready before you start stir-frying – they should be cut evenly and finely.

**Shallow frying** You can use your wok for most of the shallow frying normally carried out in a frying pan. However it is sometimes better to use an ordinary frying pan – for example, several eggs cannot be fried together in the wok!

**Deep frying** Because of its shape the wok is not ideal for deep frying loads of chips and *it should not be used as a substitute for the western form of deep frying pan.* However, it is useful for frying small individual items of food, as the well of the wok gives a good depth of fat even if only a small amount is used.

**Braising** The wok, with its domed lid, is ideal for braising foods, both large and small. The dish remains moist and quite large quantities can be cooked in this way – even whole birds can be braised in the wok.

**Steaming** The wok makes a wonderful steamer. With the steaming rack in place,

puddings, fish, meat and rice can be steamed. The domed lid allows plenty of room for the food dishes or basins to stand on the rack and it also helps the steam to condense quickly during cooking. For long steaming the water does have to be topped up, but for shorter steaming times the moisture which runs back down into the wok is usually sufficient.

## Menu planning

Once you are used to wok cookery you won't find any problem in planning a menu around your wok. If you become really hooked on this sort of cooking you may well end up buying several woks! However, at first you may be at a loss as to what to cook in the wok and what to prepare in a separate pan.

The wok is quite large and takes up a fair amount of room on the average hob, so you really need to get the best out of it when it is hot. Each of the recipes in this book has a serving suggestion which you may like to follow and many of the dishes are planned to provide a complete meal in themselves with just a salad or some bread. When there are several dishes to be prepared in the wok for one meal, cook those which take the longest first, and cook stir-fried foods right at the last minute when you are almost ready to eat. Remember that some foods can be steamed over moist dishes which are being cooked in the well of the wok; rice, for example, can sometimes be cooked over a braised meat main course.

Electric woks can be taken to the table and the food can be cooked as you want to eat it. Serving food from your wok is one of the nicest ways of presenting it to your guests: give them bowls and chopsticks and let them delve into the pan. Remember wok cooking should be fun cooking and wok menus should be fun, not only to prepare, but also to serve.

# Soups

*The wok is not the best pan for boiling soups but it is used to prepare oriental soups and there is nothing to stop you from trying out your own favourite soup recipe in your wok if you like. However, here are just a few recipes for the sort of soups which are traditionally prepared in a wok. All these soups rely on the quality of the basic stock for their eventual flavour. In Chinese stocks pork is included with the chicken to enrich the flavour, and the result is excellent. The soup should be served in small bowls with Chinese porcelain spoons to scoop it up. Prawn crackers, available in packets from most supermarkets, make a good accompaniment for these soups.*

*For a little light-hearted and incredibly delicious entertainment there is also a recipe for a mixed soup pot. In this recipe the wok of simmering soup is taken to the table and people cook small portions of food in it as they want to eat – it is really a type of oriental fondue and it makes a splendid meal.*

# Rich Chicken Stock

*Well-flavoured chicken stock is the essential basic ingredient for most soups and many sauces. Pork is used in this recipe to enrich the stock; you can use any cut – I chose the leanest belly of pork I could find because that was the cheapest. Pork spare ribs give the stock an excellent flavour and they can be fried or grilled with seasonings and spices afterwards if you like.*

| | |
|---|---|
| 2 chicken joints | large bay leaf |
| 225 g/8 oz belly of pork (pick out the leanest you can find) | 6 peppercorns |
| 1 large onion | about 1.4 litres/2½ pints water |

Place the chicken joints in the wok. Cut the pork into cubes and cut the onion into chunks, then place both in the wok with the chicken. Add the bay leaf and peppercorns and pour in the water, adding a little extra, if necessary, just to cover the meats. Bring to the boil and skim off any scum which rises to the surface. Put the lid on the wok and reduce the heat so that the stock simmers steadily. Cook for an hour.

Lift the chicken joints out of the stock and cut all the meat off. Chop this and reserve for use in the soup, or for another purpose. Remove and discard the onion, pork and bay leaf, then strain the stock through a piece of fine muslin or a coffee filter paper. If the stock looks greasy, then chill it thoroughly and skim off the fat. The stock is now ready for use, but remember that it is not seasoned.

A simple chicken soup can be prepared by returning the chopped chicken to the stock and adding seasoning to taste. Heat through and sprinkle some chopped parsley into the light broth. This is excellent for slimmers.

The stock can be kept in the refrigerator for a few days, or it can be frozen for later use. MAKES 900 ml/1½ pints

# Egg Drop Soup

*This widely known Chinese soup is easily prepared and the wok is ideal for doing so because it gives a large surface area of soup into which the beaten egg can be swirled. The success of this soup depends on the quality of the stock, so don't cut corners and try to use a cube.*

900 ml/1½ pints Rich Chicken
Stock (page 17)
6 spring onions
2 tablespoons chopped fresh
coriander leaves
about 4 tablespoons soy sauce

salt and freshly ground black
pepper
2 teaspoons cornflour
1 tablespoon cold water
2 eggs

Prepare the stock according to the recipe instructions, straining it and removing any excess fat if necessary. Stir in the chopped chicken meat. Finely chop the spring onions and mix them with the coriander.

Pour the stock into the wok and heat through, then stir in the soy sauce, tasting the soup as you do so, and add seasoning to taste. The soup will need some pepper but, depending on the strength of the soy sauce, it may not need any salt. Blend the cornflour with the water and stir into the hot soup, then bring to the boil to thicken slightly.

Beat the eggs thoroughly without allowing them to become frothy – the idea is to combine the yolks and whites evenly. Stir the spring onion mixture into the soup, bring to a rapid boil and stir the soup so that it swirls around vigorously in the wok. Immediately turn off the heat and pour in the egg in a slow thin stream. It should set in the swirling soup to give thin strips. Serve straightaway. SERVES 4

# Chicken and Sweet Corn Soup

*Illustrated on page 12*

*Serve crisp prawn crackers to complement this soup.*

900 ml/1½ pints Rich Chicken
Stock (page 17)
350 g/12 oz sweet corn
salt and freshly ground black
pepper

2 teaspoons cornflour (optional)
1 tablespoon water (optional)
chopped spring onions to garnish
(optional)

Prepare the stock according to the recipe instructions, straining it and removing any excess fat if necessary. Pour the stock into the wok and add 225 g/8 oz of the sweet corn. Bring to the boil, add seasoning and simmer for 15 minutes with the lid on the wok. Blend the soup in a liquidiser until smooth, then return it to the wok.

Reheat the soup and decide whether it is thick enough for your liking. If not, blend the cornflour with the water and stir it into the soup, then bring to the boil. Add the remaining sweet corn and the chopped chicken reserved from preparing the stock. Simmer for 5 minutes, then taste and adjust the seasoning before serving, garnished with spring onions if you like. SERVES 4

# Wun Tun Soup

*This is a delicious and filling soup. Serve it in Chinese bowls and give your guests Chinese spoons, and chopsticks for picking up the wun tuns.*

900 ml/1½ pints Rich Chicken
Stock (page 17)
1 quantity Pork Wun Tuns –
dough and filling (page 94)
about 4 tablespoons soy sauce

GARNISH
2 tablespoons chopped spring
onion
2 tablespoons chopped canned
pimiento

Prepare the stock according to the recipe instructions, straining it and removing the fat if necessary. You do not require the chopped chicken meat for this recipe, so reserve that for another use. Prepare the wun tun dough and filling and make up the wun tuns according to the recipe instructions.

Pour the stock into the wok and heat through, then add the soy sauce, tasting the soup as you do so, until it is seasoned to your liking. The amount of sauce needed will depend on its strength – some varieties are more salty than others. Bring the soup to the boil, then reduce the heat so that it simmers steadily and gradually add the wun tuns. Simmer for 5 minutes, moving the wun tuns around in the soup as they cook to prevent them from sticking together.

If you are taking the wok to the table sprinkle the garnish over the soup. Alternatively, use a slotted spoon to transfer the wun tuns to warmed bowls, then ladle the soup over them and garnish before serving. SERVES 4

*Top:* Cidered Haddock (page 30); *bottom:* Celery-stuffed Cod (page 28)

# Spinach and Bean Curd Soup

*Illustrated on page 12*

*This is another recipe which relies on the quality of the stock for its success.
Serve crisp fried noodles or prawn crackers to add variety of texture when
you make this soup.*

900 ml/1½ pints Rich Chicken
Stock (page 17)
450 g/1 lb fresh spinach
225 g/8 oz bean curd
1 bunch spring onions
2 green chillies

1 red pepper
salt and freshly ground black
pepper
1 tablespoon cornflour
2 tablespoons water

Prepare the stock according to the recipe instructions, straining it and
removing excess fat if necessary. Thoroughly wash and finely shred the
spinach, removing any large stalks as you do so. Slice the bean curd and chop
the spring onions. Remove the stalks from the chillies and discard all the
seeds from inside, then slice the green part into rings. Cut the stalk end off
the red pepper and remove all the pith and seeds from inside, then halve the
flesh and cut it into fine strips.

Pour the stock into the wok and bring to the boil. Add the chillies and red
pepper, and seasoning to taste, then simmer for 5 minutes. Stir in the spinach
and spring onions and cook for a further 2 to 3 minutes. Meanwhile, blend
the cornflour with the water until smooth, then stir this into the soup. Bring
to the boil, simmer for 2 minutes, then stir in the chopped chicken reserved
from making the stock, and the bean curd. Heat through without boiling,
then serve from the wok or ladle into individual bowls. SERVES 4

*Top:* Paupiettes Florentine (page 38); *bottom:* Plaice Goujons with Vegetables
(page 41)

# Mixed Soup Pot

*Illustrated on page 10*

*To be correct, this soup pot should be prepared in a Mongolian fire pot, so if you have one this is your chance to use it! This recipe is the oriental answer to the fondue, and it works perfectly well in the wok provided you read these few guidelines.*

*You can only prepare this recipe in your wok if you have some form of table burner on which you can safely stand the wok – the idea is included because it is great fun to cook individual portions of food in this way at the table. I have a fondue burner which has a removable rack covering the flames, and on which the fondue pan normally sits. When the rack is removed the wok sits neatly over the flames in the metal frame. This way I can take the wok to the table with no fear of it overbalancing during the meal. An electric wok is, of course, ideal for preparing this recipe – use an extension lead if necessary and keep the wire safely tucked away.*

*Serve all the uncooked foods neatly arranged and garnished and provide small bowls, chopsticks, spoons and plenty of table napkins for your guests. There are several sauce accompaniments given below – serve them if you like – and prepare a large bowl of steamed or boiled rice. When everyone has eaten their fill, any remaining ingredients are put into the wok, cooked for a few minutes, then the soup is ladled into the bowls and eaten to complete the meal.*

900 ml/1½ pints Rich Chicken
Stock (page 17)
1 small Chinese cabbage
1 bunch spring onions
1 red pepper
150 ml/¼ pint dry sherry
about 300 ml/½ pint water
salt and freshly ground black
pepper
TO COOK AT THE TABLE
1 quantity Pork Wun Tuns –
dough and filling (page 94)

4 plaice fillets
225 g/8 oz fillet steak
2 small chicken breasts
1 clove garlic
2 tablespoons soy sauce
225 g/8 oz peeled cooked
prawns
4 Chinese sausages (optional)
GARNISH
1 bunch radishes
1 lemon
fresh coriander leaves

First prepare the stock according to the recipe instructions, straining it and removing any excess fat if necessary. Pour it into the wok and add the reserved, chopped, cooked chicken meat.

Shred the Chinese cabbage and chop two of the spring onions, then add these to the stock. Cut the stalk end off the red pepper and remove all the seeds and pith from inside, then halve the flesh and cut it into fine strips. Add these to the wok. Pour in the sherry and water – you may need to add more water later at the end of the meal; it depends on how long it takes to cook and eat all the food and how much liquid evaporates during cooking. Add seasoning to taste – do not be over generous as the soup may become too salty later on.

Now prepare the ingredients for cooking at the table. You do not have to present a wide variety of foods – if you like you can have just one sort of fish and some meat. Adjust the quantities accordingly but remember that people tend to eat far more at this type of meal than they would normally!

Prepare the wun tun dough and filling according to the recipe instructions. Place a teaspoon or so of filling in the centre of each wun tun skin. Bring opposite corners together over the filling and seal the edges firmly. Fold the remaining two corners towards each other, to form a shape resembling a mitre, and seal. Skin the fish fillets (see Paupiettes Florentine, page 38) and cut the flesh into strips. Place the fillet steak in the freezer until it is half frozen, then cut it into very thin slices – use a very sharp knife to do this, but if you don't feel confident that you will actually end up with fine slices, then try cutting the meat into fine strips. Cut the chicken breasts into fine slices and place them in a small bowl, then crush the garlic over the chicken and sprinkle the soy sauce over too. Stir to coat the chicken in the flavouring ingredients, then leave to marinate for several hours. Slice the sausages diagonally, if using.

It is important whenever you present raw foods at the table to make sure they are attractively garnished – the garnish needn't be elaborate, just neat and simple. Make the remaining spring onions into curls (see Meatballs with Prawns, page 86) and trim the radishes. Make crossways slits down through the radishes to give several small wedges, leaving them attached at the base. Open the wedges out slightly to form flower shapes. Slice the lemon and cut the slices in half. Arrange all the prepared foods on dishes and garnish with the prepared ingredients and with a few leaves of fresh coriander.

Bring the soup in the wok to the boil on the cooker hob. Have ready the burner on a heatproof mat on the table. Boil the soup for 2 minutes, then take the wok to the table. Arrange all the dishes around the wok and encourage your guests to help themselves to the morsels of food, using chopsticks, fondue forks or special individual draining baskets to dip the food into the simmering soup. Most of the foods will cook in 1 or 2 minutes; the wun tuns will take 5 minutes – these can be dropped into the soup a few at a time and people can fish them out when they are ready. The cooked foods can be dipped into any of the sauces suggested below, if you like, and eaten with boiled rice.

When all the foods are eaten, or when you are nearly full, put any remaining pieces into the soup. Have a quick taste to make sure that the soup has not become too concentrated and add a little extra water if you like. Heat through for a few minutes, then ladle the soup into bowls and eat it to round off the meal. SERVES 4

# Chilli Garlic Dip

3 cloves garlic, crushed
2 tablespoons chilli sauce

2 tablespoons soy sauce

Mix all the ingredients together and place the dip in a small dish. Tiny amounts of this dip are required to flavour foods.

# Quick Plum Dip

100 g/4 oz plum jam (choose a
good quality preserve)
2 tablespoons wine vinegar

2 cloves garlic, crushed
pinch of chilli powder

Mix all the ingredients and spoon the dip into a bowl.

# Spicy Peanut Dip

100 g/4 oz salted peanuts
2 cloves garlic
$\frac{1}{2}$ teaspoon chilli powder
2 tablespoons lemon juice

a few drops of sesame oil
100 ml/4 fl oz oil
soy sauce

Grind the peanuts in a liquidiser with the garlic, chilli powder and lemon juice. When the peanuts are reduced to a very coarse paste add the sesame oil and continue blending the mixture, pouring in the 100 ml/4 fl oz of oil in a slow stream. Blend until smooth, then season to taste with soy sauce.

# Water Chestnut and Onion Dip

100 g/4 oz salted cashew nuts
150 ml/$\frac{1}{4}$ pint unsweetened
apple juice
1 onion
1 (227-g/8-oz) can water chestnuts,
drained

2 tablespoons chopped fresh
coriander leaves
soy sauce

Place the nuts and apple juice in a liquidiser and blend until they form a smooth cream. Chop the onion and water chestnuts very finely and stir them into the cream with the coriander and soy sauce to taste. Chill lightly before serving.

# Fish and Seafood

*The wok is ideal for cooking fish and seafood because these are foods which taste their very best when cooked quickly. Whether steamed, braised or fried, wok-cooked fish taste simply splendid.*

*The recipes in this chapter range from quick and economical dishes which are ideal for feeding the family, to more sophisticated ideas for when you're entertaining friends. There are some oriental dishes — Fish with Black Bean Sauce, for example — and some for fish and shellfish cooked in curry spices. Cooking in a wok always seems to invite a touch of the unusual, so why not experiment with some of the lesser known fish that can be found occasionally? Try, for example, using shark cutlets, or chunks of this meaty fish, in recipes which are highly spiced — Fish Curry or Prawn Curry for example — you may well find the result very pleasing. And some of the more common fish like mullet can be cooked whole on the steaming rack in the wok: well seasoned and wrapped in foil, the cooked fish is exceptionally moist and well flavoured.*

*Think of your wok as an exciting international cooking pan and use your imagination when cooking in it.*

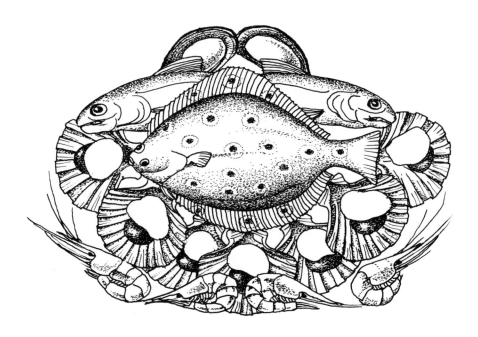

# Celery-stuffed Cod

*Illustrated on page 21*

*The combination of a substantial stuffing and braised vegetables make this dish quite filling. Serve thickly sliced Granary bread or French bread, a salad or some boiled new potatoes as accompaniments.*

2 sticks celery
1 small onion
2 rashers streaky bacon, rind removed
50 g/2 oz fresh breadcrumbs
salt and freshly ground black pepper
2 cod steaks
50 g/2 oz butter
milk
350 g/12 oz new carrots
bay leaf
300 ml/$\frac{1}{2}$ pint dry white wine
150 ml/$\frac{1}{4}$ pint water
2 egg yolks
4 tablespoons double cream
chopped parsley to garnish

Finely chop the celery, onion and streaky bacon. Place the breadcrumbs in a bowl with plenty of seasoning. Remove the central bones from the cod steaks and set the steaks aside on a large piece of buttered foil.

Melt the butter in the wok, add the celery, onion and bacon, and cook, stirring continuously, until the onion is soft and the bacon cooked. Add the cooked mixture to the breadcrumbs and stir well, then pour in just enough milk to bind the ingredients together. Divide this stuffing between the cod steaks, pressing it well into the cavities left by the bones.

Add the carrots to the wok and throw in the bay leaf, then pour in the wine and water. Stand the steaming rack over the vegetables and heat to boiling point. Reduce the heat. Pack the fish closely in the foil, making sure that the edges are well sealed, and place the package on the steaming rack. Put the lid on the wok and simmer gently for 20 minutes. By this time most of the liquid will have evaporated from the vegetables; they will be cooked and the fish will be ready to serve. Transfer the fish to a heated serving dish and, using a draining spoon, lift the carrots out of the liquid. Arrange them round the fish.

Whisk the egg yolks with the cream and stir them into the liquid left in the wok. Heat very gently without allowing the sauce to boil (it will curdle if overheated) then pour it over the fish. Sprinkle a little chopped parsley over the fish before serving. SERVES 2

# Bass Boulangère

*I used bass for this recipe because I am lucky enough to have a father-in-law who goes sea fishing and kindly shares the fruits of his day's sport. Bass is a delicately flavoured, firm fish with very large bones which are easily removed; it is available on occasions from fishmongers, but is not as common as cod or haddock, which can be substituted in this recipe if you like.*

| | |
|---|---|
| 1 kg/2 lb bass fillets | freshly ground black pepper |
| 675 g/1½ lb potatoes | 2 sprigs rosemary |
| ½ lemon | a few extra sprigs of rosemary to |
| 50 g/2 oz butter | garnish |
| garlic salt | |

Cut the fish into two portions if the fillet is in one piece, then remove the skin (see Paupiettes Florentine, page 38). Remove any stray bones which have not been discarded in the filleting. Thinly slice the potatoes. Squeeze the juice from the lemon half. Cut the lemon shell into quarters, then scrape out any pips.

Melt half the butter in the wok and make sure that it is well swirled around the sides. Add the potatoes in two layers, spinkling them with garlic salt and pepper. Lay the fish on top of the potatoes and sprinkle more seasoning over, then pour in the lemon juice and dot with the remaining butter. Arrange the rosemary sprigs and lemon shell pieces on or around the fish and put the lid on the wok. Simmer gently for 30 to 40 minutes, or until the potatoes are tender and the fish is cooked.

Serve the fish immediately, with the pieces of lemon and a few fresh sprigs of rosemary arranged as a garnish on the top. SERVES 4

# Cidered Haddock

*Illustrated on page 21*

*The wok is ideal for poaching fillets of larger fish because they do not usually fit into an average frying pan unless they are cut up. This very simple dish is delicious: the tangy cider complements the fish very well. Serve it with boiled rice, creamed or baked potatoes, or buttered new potatoes.*

4 medium-sized haddock fillets
1 large onion
1 green pepper
2 carrots
50 g/2 oz butter *or* 2 tablespoons oil
2 tablespoons plain flour

salt and freshly ground black pepper
600 ml/1 pint dry cider
bay leaf
4 tablespoons chopped parsley
100 g/4 oz sweet corn

Skin the fish fillets (see Paupiettes Florentine, page 38). Thinly slice the onion. Cut the stalk end off the green pepper and remove all the seeds and pith from inside, then slice the green flesh. Thinly slice the carrots.

Melt the butter or heat the oil in the wok and add the onion and green pepper, then fry, turning the slices frequently, until the onion has softened. Stir in the flour and seasoning and cook for a minute, then pour in the cider and add the bay leaf, parsley and carrots. Bring to the boil, reduce the heat so that the sauce simmers and slide the fish into the wok. Put the lid on and cook for 30 minutes. Sprinkle the sweet corn into the wok for the last 5 minutes of cooking time.

Serve immediately, straight from the wok if you like, or carefully transferred to a heated serving platter or dish. SERVES 4

# Coley with Corn Sauce

*So many people think of coley as being fit only for the cat — but that really isn't true. The fish has a coarse texture and tough skin which must be removed before cooking, but its flavour is not overpoweringly strong and it tastes very good combined with the right sauce. Serve this dish with confidence (don't tell your guests or family if you think they will be fussy) but it's not quite enough on its own so have a bowl of buttered rice or pasta ready as well.*

675 g/1½ lb coley fillets
2 onions
50 g/2 oz butter *or* 2 tablespoons oil
2 cloves garlic
grated rind and juice of 1 orange
bay leaf
2 tablespoons plain flour

salt and freshly ground black pepper
2 (397-g/14-oz) cans tomatoes
150 ml/¼ pint chicken stock
225 g/8 oz sweet corn
GARNISH
1 orange
watercress sprigs

Skin the coley (see Paupiettes Florentine, page 38) and remove any bones from the flesh, then cut the fish into chunks. Chop the onions.

Melt the butter or heat the oil in the wok and add the onions, then crush the garlic into the pan and stir in the orange rind and bay leaf. Fry until the onions are soft but not browned, then add the fish and cook for a few minutes. Sprinkle in the flour, add seasoning and cook for a minute. Pour in the tomatoes and break them up slightly in the wok, then add the stock and orange juice. Bring to the boil, reduce the heat and simmer gently for 30 minutes. Stir in the sweet corn and simmer for a further 10 minutes.

While the fish is cooking, slice the orange for garnish. Serve the fish straight from the wok or on a bed of cooked rice or pasta, garnished with orange slices and watercress sprigs. SERVES 4

# Crunchy-topped Coley

*Illustrated on page 40*

*This is an economical recipe for those useful pre-formed fish steaks which
have no skin or bones to worry about. Serve baked potatoes as an
accompaniment if you want a substantial meal, or offer a green salad and
some crusty bread for a lighter result.*

4 coley steaks
salt and freshly ground black
pepper
2 tablespoons plain flour
4 slices bread
4 tomatoes
2 sticks celery

50 g/2 oz black olives (optional)
2 cloves garlic
50 g/2 oz butter
2 tablespoons oil
chopped parsley to garnish
(optional)

There is no need to defrost the fish steaks: simply sprinkle them with plenty
of seasoning and dust them with flour.

Cut the crusts off the bread and cut the slices into neat cubes. Place the
tomatoes in a bowl and cover them with boiling water, leave to stand for
about 30 seconds, then drain and peel them. Cut the peeled tomatoes into
eighths. Thinly slice the celery, and stone the olives if using.

Crush the garlic into the wok and add the butter and oil. Heat gently until
the butter melts, then increase the heat and add the cubes of bread. Fry these
on all sides until golden, then remove from the wok and drain on absorbent
kitchen paper.

Add the fish to the fat remaining in the pan and fry on both sides until
golden brown and cooked. Remove from the wok and place on a heated
serving dish; keep hot.

Add the celery to the wok and stir over a high heat for a minute. Then add
the tomatoes, and the olives if using, and cook for a few minutes more. Taste
and adjust the seasoning. Spoon this mixture over the fish in the serving dish
and top with the bread croûtons, then sprinkle with chopped parsley and
serve immediately.

Alternatively, the fish steaks can be returned to the wok, arranged neatly
on the vegetables, topped with the croûtons, then garnished for serving
straight from the pan. SERVES 4

# Fish with Black Bean Sauce

*Black bean sauce is a traditional accompaniment to fish and chicken in oriental dishes; it is rich and delicious. Salted black beans are small wrinkled black beans with a pungent, salty taste. They are sold in packets or they are sometimes described as fermented beans and sold in cans; they can be obtained from oriental supermarkets or delicatessen shops.*

25 g/1 oz fresh root ginger
4 large spring onions
1 large clove garlic
sesame oil
3 tablespoons salted black beans
1 tablespoon lemon juice
2 tablespoons soy sauce

2 teaspoons sugar
150 ml/$\frac{1}{4}$ pint dry sherry
675 g/$1\frac{1}{2}$ lb white fish fillet, in two thick pieces (for example, cod, haddock or coley)
1 red pepper, cut into fine strips, to garnish

Scrub the ginger, then cut it into very fine strips. Cut the spring onions diagonally into fine strips and chop the garlic. Heat a little oil in the wok and add the ginger and garlic, with the black beans. Stir-fry for a few minutes, then stir in the lemon juice, soy sauce, sugar and sherry.

Skin the fish (see Paupiettes Florentine, page 38) and lay the fillets in the sauce in the wok. Simmer gently for 20 to 25 minutes, by which time the fish should be cooked through. Sprinkle the spring onions over the top of the fish, cook for just a few minutes longer, then tranfer to a heated serving dish. Serve immediately, garnished with the red pepper strips. SERVES 4

**Note** The black bean sauce can be used as a cooking medium for chicken or prawns. Prepare thin slices of uncooked chicken, or use peeled cooked prawns, and simmer them in the sauce as above.

# Fish Curry

*Here is a very simple recipe for a fish curry – serve boiled rice and papadums, mango chutney and lime pickle as accompaniments. If you like, you can also serve small bowls of chopped tomatoes, cucumber, green peppers and hard-boiled eggs.*

1 kg/2 lb white fish fillets (for example, haddock, cod, coley or cod cheeks)
2 onions
3 tablespoons oil
4 cloves garlic
1 teaspoon ground ginger
$\frac{1}{2}$ teaspoon turmeric
2 tablespoons garam masala

$\frac{1}{2}$–2 teaspoons chilli powder, or to taste (you may like to omit this completely)
salt and freshly ground black pepper
2 tablespoons plain flour
600 ml/1 pint hot water
100 g/4 oz coconut cream
chopped fresh coriander leaves to garnish

Skin the fish fillets (see Paupiettes Florentine, page 38) and cut the flesh into chunks. Slice the onions thinly.

Heat the oil in the wok and add the onions, then crush the garlic cloves into the pan. Fry until the onions are soft but not browned. Add the spices, taking care with the chilli powder unless you like hot curries, then add salt and pepper to taste. Cook for a few minutes before stirring in the chunks of fish and the flour. Pour in half the water and bring to the boil, then simmer for 5 minutes.

Meanwhile, dissolve the coconut cream in the remaining water. Pour this over the fish and bring back to a simmer. Put the lid on the wok and cook for a further 20 minutes, then serve, garnished with the fresh coriander.
SERVES 4

# Oriental Fishballs

*Serve this fish and vegetable dish with rice or chow mein noodles to complete the meal.*

450 g/1 lb white fish
5 tablespoons soy sauce
1 generous tablespoon plain flour
4 dried Chinese mushrooms
1 small onion

2 pieces canned bamboo shoot
450 g/1 lb Chinese cabbage
oil for frying
4 tablespoons dry sherry

Skin the fish (see Paupiettes Florentine, page 38) and chop the flesh, removing any bones. Mix the chopped fish with a scant tablespoon of the soy sauce and with the flour, then pound the ingredients thoroughly until they are combined. Take small spoonfuls of the fish mixture and knead it into balls in the palms of your hands.

Place the mushrooms in a small basin and pour on sufficient boiling water to cover. Leave to soak for 20 minutes. Halve and finely slice the onion and finely slice the pieces of bamboo shoot. Shred the cabbage and mix it with the bamboo shoots. Drain the soaked mushrooms and slice them too.

Heat the oil in the wok and add the fishballs, then fry, turning carefully, until golden brown on all sides. Remove them from the wok and drain on absorbent kitchen paper. Add the onion and mushrooms to the oil remaining in the wok and stir-fry for a few minutes, then add the cabbage and bamboo shoots and continue to cook for a minute. Pour in the remaining soy sauce and the sherry. Replace the fishballs on top of the vegetables and put the lid on the wok, then cook over medium heat for 2 to 3 minutes. Serve immediately, straight from the wok if you like. SERVES 4

# Saucy Crisp Whiting

*The wok is useful for preparing simple fried foods as well as for experimenting with more adventurous ethnic dishes. Here, simple breaded fish fillets are fried in the wok and a sauce of peppers and tomatoes is heated through to complement them.*

| | |
|---|---|
| 4 large whiting fillets | 1 (200-g/7-oz) can sweet red |
| 4 tablespoons plain flour | peppers |
| salt and freshly ground black | 50 g/2 oz butter |
| pepper | 1 (397-g/14-oz) can tomatoes |
| 1 egg, lightly beaten | 2 tablespoons capers |
| 100 g/4 oz dry white breadcrumbs | 1 tablespoon whole grain mustard |

Coat the whiting fillets in the flour and sprinkle them generously with salt and pepper. Dip the fillets first in the egg, then in the breadcrumbs, pressing them on well. Drain and chop the sweet peppers.

Melt the butter in the wok and add the fish, then fry until golden on the underside. Turn over and fry the second side; the coating should be crisp and golden. Drain on absorbent kitchen paper and arrange on a heated serving dish.

Add the peppers to the butter remaining in the wok, then stir in all the remaining ingredients and season to taste. Heat through to boiling point and pour over the fish. Serve straightaway, so that the crisp coating retains its texture. SERVES 4

# Steamed Plaice

*Steamed fish with ginger and lemon grass is moist and very well flavoured. Ask your fishmonger to remove the head and the small amount of gut from the plaice. Serve with simple steamed or boiled rice.*

2 whole plaice, heads removed
and gutted
4 slices fresh root ginger
2 large stalks lemon grass

3 tablespoons soy sauce
GARNISH
1 lemon, sliced
$\frac{1}{4}$ cucumber, sliced

Rinse and dry the fish, then make a neat slit down the centre of the back bone and cut between the bone and the flesh, working outwards to make a large pocket on each side. Place the ginger slices and lemon grass in the pockets, allowing two slices of ginger and a piece of lemon grass for each fish.

Lay the fish on a large plate and sprinkle over the soy sauce. Alternatively, wrap the soy sauce-coated fish in greased foil. Place on the steaming rack in the wok and add water to come up to the edge of the rack. Bring to the boil and put the lid on the wok, then steam for 15 to 20 minutes, or until the plaice is cooked through.

Garnish the cooked fish with sliced lemon and cucumber and serve immediately. SERVES 4

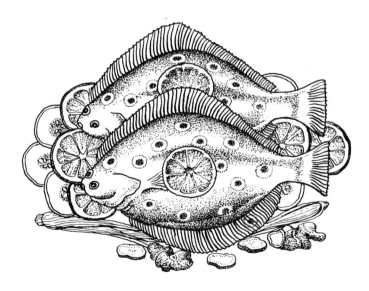

# Paupiettes Florentine

*Illustrated on page 22*

*Whereas most frying pans are only large enough to cook a few rolls of fish at a time, the wok is big enough to enable eight fillets of plaice to be cooked at once. Combined with a garnish of crisp fried potatoes this dish can be served with either a salad or some lightly boiled French beans or peas to make a complete meal.*

8 large plaice fillets
salt and freshly ground black
pepper
1 (300-g/10.6-oz) packet frozen
chopped spinach, thawed
50 g/2 oz Emmental cheese, grated
freshly grated nutmeg

675 g/1½ lb potatoes
grated rind of 1 lemon
2 tablespoons oil
50 g/2 oz butter
parsley sprigs to garnish
(optional)

First skin the fish fillets. Place the fillets on a board, skin side down, and rub your fingers in a little salt. Holding the tail end of each fillet firmly between your salted fingers, use a sharp knife to cut between the skin and the flesh of the fish. Hold the knife at an acute angle to the board and use a slight sawing motion to ease the flesh off the skin without puncturing the skin at all.

Mix the thoroughly drained spinach with the cheese, nutmeg and plenty of salt and pepper. Spread a little of this mixture over each fish fillet and roll them up to enclose the filling. Use wooden cocktail sticks to secure the rolls.

Cut the potatoes into small even dice and mix them with the lemon rind. Heat the oil and butter together in the wok, add the fish rolls and fry them until browned all over. Remove the fish from the pan. Add the potatoes to the fat remaining in the wok and cook over high heat until golden brown all over. Place the steaming rack over the potatoes and reduce the heat under the wok. Arrange the fish on the rack and put the lid on the wok. Cook gently for 15 minutes.

Carefully lift the fish off the rack, then arrange the rolls in a heated serving dish. Spoon the potatoes around the fish and garnish with parsley sprigs, if liked, before serving. SERVES 4

Prawn Curry with (*left*) Radish and Pepper Raita (page 47); *right:* Fresh Mango Relish (page 164)

# Plaice Goujons with Vegetables

*Illustrated on page 22*

*The crisp sticks of fried fish go very well with stir-fried vegetables in this recipe. Serve the sauce separately, in a small dish, and offer warm pita bread or pumpernickel as an accompaniment.*

8 plaice fillets
3 tablespoons plain flour
salt and freshly ground black
pepper
1 egg, beaten
75 g/3 oz fine dry breadcrumbs
3 sticks celery
100 g/4 oz carrots
1 red pepper
1 small onion

2 tablespoons oil
SAUCE
2 tablespoons chopped capers
2 tablespoons chopped parsley
1 teaspoon grated lemon rind
150 ml/$\frac{1}{4}$ pint mayonnaise
150 ml/$\frac{1}{4}$ pint soured cream
salt and freshly ground black
pepper

Skin the plaice fillets (see Paupiettes Florentine, page 38) and cut the flesh into fine strips. Mix the flour with the seasoning on a plate or in a polythene bag. Coat the fish strips in the seasoned flour, either by rolling them on the plate or by shaking them in the bag. Dip the fish first in the beaten egg, then in the breadcrumbs, pressing them on well. Place the strips in the refrigerator while you prepare the vegetables.

Finely slice the celery and carrots. Cut the stalk end off the pepper and remove the seeds and pith from inside, then cut the flesh into thin slices. Halve and slice the onion.

Heat the oil in the wok, add the fish strips and fry them, turning once or twice, until golden and crisp. Drain on absorbent kitchen paper and set aside to keep hot. Add the prepared vegetables to the fat remaining in the wok and stir-fry them until they are just tender. Arrange the vegetables on a heated serving dish, or leave them in the wok and place the fish goujons on top.

To make the sauce, mix the capers, parsley and lemon rind into the mayonnaise. Stir in the soured cream and season to taste. Serve the fish and vegetables, with the sauce handed separately in a small bowl. SERVES 4

*Top:* Crunchy-topped Coley (page 32); *bottom:* Trout with Courgettes
(page 45)

# Five-spice Fish

*Serve this deliciously spiced mackerel with an oriental salad – a mixture of shredded water chestnuts, bamboo shoots and Chinese cabbage with bean sprouts and spring onions. Dress the salad with a few drops of sesame oil mixed with a crushed clove of garlic, some corn oil and a little lemon juice.*

4 small mackerel, gutted
1 tablespoon plain flour
½ teaspoon five spice powder
2 tablespoons oil
1 stick celery

pared rind of 1 small lemon
1 tablespoon soy sauce
a few spring onions, chopped, to garnish

Cut off and discard the heads from the fish, then open out the fish and press them flat. Rinse the mackerel and dry them on absorbent kitchen paper.

To bone the mackerel – or any other round fish of this type, such as a herring – lay the fish flat on a board with the skin side uppermost. Press firmly down the length of the back bone, then turn the fish over and lift off the bones which should be freed from the flesh. Remove any stray bones and the fish is ready for use.

Mix the flour with the five spice powder and sprinkle this over the flesh of the mackerel. Heat the oil in the wok and place the fish in the pan, arranging them so that they all fit neatly around the sides. Cook until brown and crisp underneath, turning them round once to ensure that they cook evenly. Then turn the fish over and cook the second side until brown and crisp.

Meanwhile, cut the celery into fine strips and cut the lemon rind into similar-sized pieces. Transfer the cooked fish to a heated serving dish and add the celery and lemon rind to the fat remaining in the pan. Stir-fry quickly for a few minutes, then sprinkle in the soy sauce and top the fish with this mixture. Garnish with spring onions and serve immediately.
SERVES 4

## Five spice powder

This can be obtained from Chinese supermarkets, delicatessen shops or good supermarkets. It is a mixture of ground spices consisting of peppercorns, star anise, fennel seeds, cinnamon and cloves. A small quantity is usually enough to flavour most dishes.

# Seafood Special

*You can add whatever seafood you like to this dish — it is really just a simple seafood stew. Add cooked crab, cockles or scallops, for example, and use any white fish of your choice as the base — cod or haddock give a particularly good texture. Serve the fish straight from the wok, with a salad of mixed green vegetables (to include finely sliced peppers, chicory and spring onions) and plenty of warm French bread and butter.*

450 g/1 lb white fish fillets
1 onion
1 (105-g/3.66-oz) can smoked oysters
4 slices white bread
1 tablespoon oil
50 g/2 oz butter
1 clove garlic
salt and freshly ground black pepper

2 tablespoons plain flour
300 ml/$\frac{1}{2}$ pint dry white wine
175 g/6 oz peeled cooked prawns
225 g/8 oz cooked mussels (do not use those which are pickled in vinegar)
100 g/4 oz small button mushrooms
150 ml/$\frac{1}{4}$ pint double cream
4 tablespoons chopped parsley

Skin the fish (see Paupiettes Florentine, page 38) and remove any stray bones, then cut the fish into chunks. Thinly slice the onion and drain the oysters. Cut the crusts off the bread and cut the slices into small cubes to make crisp croûtons to garnish the cooked stew.

Heat the oil with half the butter in the wok and add the bread cubes, tossing them well in the fat to coat them evenly. Fry, turning frequently, until the cubes are golden brown, then remove them from the wok and drain on absorbent kitchen paper.

Add the remaining butter to the wok and crush the garlic into it. Stir in the onion and add plenty of seasoning, then cook until soft but not browned. Sprinkle in the flour and cook for a minute, then add the wine and bring to the boil. Reduce the heat and add the prepared fish, spooning the sauce over it. Simmer for 15 minutes before adding the prawns, mussels and mushrooms, then continue to cook at a simmer for a further 5 minutes. Now add the oysters and stir in the cream, heat gently without boiling and stir in the parsley.

Sprinkle the croûtons over the fish as soon as the sauce is heated through and serve immediately — before the bread has time to become soggy!
SERVES 4

# Scallops in Lemon Cream Sauce

*Scallops are one of my favourite shellfish and, although they seem expensive when priced up on the fishmonger's counter, they do go a long way. If you want a real feast you can, of course, add a few more scallops to the quantities given below. I have prepared yellow rice to complete the meal but this is optional; if you like, serve the cooked scallops, with the lemon cream poured over and warmed, with plenty of crisp French bread or brown bread and butter. Whichever you decide, a fresh green salad (with lots of variety in the ingredients) will go down very well as an accompaniment.*

| | |
|---|---|
| 12 large prepared scallops | $\frac{1}{4}$ teaspoon turmeric |
| 4 rashers lean bacon | bay leaf |
| 1 small onion | 600 ml/1 pint water |
| 100 g/4 oz butter | grated rind of 1 lemon |
| salt and freshly ground black pepper | 150 ml/$\frac{1}{4}$ pint soured cream |
| 225 g/8 oz long-grain rice | 4 tablespoons chopped parsley |

Slice the scallops thickly. Cut the rinds off the bacon and dice the rashers. Chop the onion finely.

Melt half the butter in the wok and add the onion, with seasoning to taste. Fry until soft. Then add the scallops and bacon and fry over medium heat until both are just cooked – do not overcook the scallops. Remove the mixture from the wok, with the buttery juices, and pour it into a basin.

Add the remaining butter to the wok and stir in the rice. Cook, stirring, for a minute, then stir in the turmeric and add the bay leaf. Pour in the water and add salt to taste. Bring to the boil, reduce the heat so that the water simmers, then put the lid on the wok and cook for 15 minutes. By this time the rice should have absorbed most of the water.

As soon as you have put the rice on to cook, stir the lemon rind and soured cream into the buttery scallops and add about half of the parsley, reserving the remainder for garnishing the dish. When the rice has cooked for 15 minutes, fork it lightly, then spoon the scallops over the middle of the rice, pouring the cream over them. Put the lid back on the wok and cook for a further 5 minutes, to warm the scallops through.

Sprinkle the reserved parsley neatly over the scallops and serve immediately, straight from the wok. If you would prefer to serve the scallops and rice from a separate serving dish, cook the rice for the full 20 minutes,

then transfer it to the heated dish. Pour the scallops and their cream sauce into the wok and heat through gently without allowing them to boil at all. Pour over the rice and sprinkle with chopped parsley before serving.
SERVES 4

**Note** This recipe is particularly rich in butter (and delicious, too) but if you would prefer a slightly less buttery dish you can omit the brief period of frying for the rice and therefore use only 50 g/2 oz butter.

# Trout with Courgettes

*Illustrated on page 40*

*It is possible to cook more than two trout in the wok at the same time, but if they are fairly large they may become slightly curved due to the shape of the wok. If you do want to prepare four fish, then brown the fish two at a time in the wok and arrange them on the steaming rack over the courgettes to finish cooking.*

50 g/2 oz butter
2 trout, gutted
4 courgettes
2 tablespoons chopped dill

salt and freshly ground black pepper
GARNISH
lemon wedges
dill sprigs

Melt the butter in the wok and add the trout. Cook until browned on the underside, then carefully turn the fish over and cook until browned on the second side. Meanwhile, slice the courgettes.

Sprinkle the courgettes over the fish in the pan. Allow as many of the slices as possible to sit beside the fish in the wok, then sprinkle the chopped dill over and add a little seasoning. Put the lid on the wok and cook gently for 20 minutes, turning the fish over after 10 minutes' cooking time.

Serve immediately on a warmed serving platter, with the courgettes arranged round the fish, garnished with lemon wedges and dill sprigs.
SERVES 2

# Moules Marinière

*The wok is excellent for preparing mussels by the traditional method of cooking them in a small amount of liquid – they are in fact steamed in the heat given off by the liquid boiling below. The curved shape of the pan and domed lid, also its large capacity, makes it a good vessel for preparing shellfish in this way. Serve the mussels in individual bowls, with the cooking liquor poured over, or be different and serve them straight from the wok! Offer French bread with the mussels.*

1.75 litres/3 pints mussels
1 onion
1 carrot
bay leaf
a few sprigs of parsley
salt and freshly ground black pepper

300 ml/½ pint dry white wine
chopped parsley to garnish
BEURRE MANIÉ
2 tablespoons plain flour
50 g/2 oz butter

Scrub the mussels thoroughly under cold running water. Remove their beards – the black hairs at the side of the shells – and make sure that the shells are clean. Discard any open shells which do not shut immediately they are tapped. Finely chop the onion and dice the carrot. Place the mussels in the wok and sprinkle over the prepared vegetables, bay leaf, sprigs of parsley and seasoning. Pour in the wine and put the wok over a high heat until the liquid boils rapidly. Put the lid on and cook over a high heat for about 5 minutes, tossing the mussels once. By this time all the shells should have opened and the mussels will be cooked. Remove the mussels from the wok, discarding any that have not opened and any empty shell halves. Keep the mussels hot while thickening the cooking liquor.

While the mussels are cooking prepare the buerre manié: gradually beat the flour into the butter, then continue creaming the mixture until it is very smooth.

Whisk small knobs of the beurre manié into the cooking liquor left in the wok. Bring to the boil, then simmer for a minute.

To serve, either pour the sauce over the mussels in individual bowls, or return the mussels to the wok and serve them straight from it. Either way, sprinkle with chopped parsley before serving. SERVES 4

# Prawn Curry

*Illustrated on page 39*

*This is excellent but rather expensive, so if you feel that you cannot stretch to serving this as a main course dish for more than two, try making half the quantity and serving it on a few crisp lettuce leaves as a starter. To complete the curry serve boiled rice, Fresh Mango Relish (page 164), Radish and Pepper Raita (below) and papadums as side dishes.*

1 large onion
2 stalks lemon grass *or* pared rind
of $\frac{1}{2}$ lemon
3 green chillies
25 g/1 oz fresh root ginger
2 cloves garlic
50 g/2 oz ghee (page 113) or butter

4 green cardamoms
1 tablespoon garam masala
salt and freshly ground black
pepper
1 kg/2 lb peeled cooked prawns
chopped fresh coriander leaves to
garnish

Finely chop the onion and cut each stalk of lemon grass into two or three pieces. Cut the stalk ends off the chillies and scoop out and discard all the seeds. Finely chop the green part and mix it with the onion and lemon grass or lemon rind. Grate the ginger and crush the garlic, and mix these together.

Melt the ghee or butter in the wok and add the onion mixture, then fry until the onion is soft but not browned. Add the ginger and garlic and cook for a further 2 to 3 minutes before stirring in the cardamoms and garam masala. Add salt and pepper to taste and continue to cook, stirring to prevent the mixture from sticking to the wok, until the cardamoms give off their appetising aroma.

Now add the prawns and toss them in the spices and juices. Put the lid on the wok and cook over a gentle heat for 3 to 5 minutes. The heat should be low enough to allow the prawns to heat through and absorb the flavour from the other ingredients without overcooking. To serve, transfer the curry to a heated serving dish or simply leave it in the wok. Sprinkle a generous amount of chopped coriander over at the last minute. SERVES 4

## Radish and Pepper Raita

1 bunch radishes
1 red pepper
1 green pepper

150 ml/$\frac{1}{4}$ pint natural yogurt
freshly grated nutmeg

Trim and thinly slice the radishes. Cut the stalk ends off the peppers and remove all their seeds and pith. Chop the pepper flesh finely and mix it with the radishes in a small bowl. Pour in the yogurt and sprinkle with freshly grated nutmeg. Chill lightly before serving.

# Butterfly Prawns
# with Hot Cucumber Sauce

*Delicious king prawns, attractively served with a flavoursome sauce, make a splendid centre-piece for any meal. Serve plenty of boiled rice to accompany this dish.*

16 cooked king prawns
plain flour
salt and freshly ground black
pepper
1 cucumber
6 green chillies
1 small onion

2 tablespoons tomato purée
1 tablespoon vinegar
1 tablespoon soft brown sugar
2 teaspoons cornflour
2 tablespoons water
75 g/3 oz butter
lemon wedges to garnish

Peel the prawns, removing their heads and body shell but leaving the end tail wings attached. Slit down the back of the prawns without cutting right through, then open out their bodies flat. Coat them in a little flour and seasoning.

Trim the ends off the cucumber and peel it very lightly, then cut it widthways into quarters. Cut the quarters into long slices, then cut the slices into fine strips. Cut the stalk ends off the chillies and remove all the seeds from inside. Cut the green part into fine strips. Thinly slice the onion and separate the slices into rings. Mix the tomato purée with the vinegar and sugar. Mix the cornflour with the water until smooth, then stir in the tomato purée mixture.

Melt the butter in the wok and fry the prawns on both sides until golden brown. Remove from the wok, drain on absorbent kitchen paper and keep hot.

Add the cucumber, onion and chillies to the butter and stir-fry until the onion has softened slightly. Pour in the sauce and bring to the boil. Taste and adjust the seasoning, then arrange the prawns on top of the sauce and garnish with the lemon wedges before serving. SERVES 4

**Right** *top:* Provençal Chicken (page 57); *bottom:* Chicken with Broccoli (page 59)
**Overleaf** *clockwise, from the top:* Fruit Pullao (page 138), Naan (page 151), Kashmiri Chicken (page 60), Okra with Tomatoes (page 112)
**Page 52** Chicken in a Wok (page 54)

# Poultry

*Poultry is no longer an expensive luxury; on the contrary, it is one of the most economical and versatile protein foods around. Chicken, for example, can be used in all sorts of dishes – in hot and hearty puddings, in light stir-fry meals – it can be crisply fried and it can also be turned into many a traditional recipe.*

*In this chapter you will find that you can cook a whole chicken in the wok with moist, tender results. Duck, too, can be casseroled for special dishes and those turkey joints that are now available all through the year can be turned into exotic specialities.*

*Hopefully, the recipes in this chapter will inspire you to experiment with the familiar chicken, and will wake you up to a whole new repertoire of exciting creations with duck and turkey too.*

# Chicken in a Wok

*Illustrated on page 52*

*I was very pleasantly surprised when I first cooked a whole chicken in my wok. Not only did the bird cook successfully without the need to top up the liquid several times during cooking, but the result was mouth-watering – tender, very well flavoured and all in just about an hour! There is no need to serve any accompaniments with this dish as the vegetables are all cooked with the chicken, although some warm Granary bread would go very well if you really do have a hungry crowd on your hands.*

1 (1.5-kg/3½-lb) oven-ready chicken
225 g/8 oz carrots
450 g/1 lb potatoes
2 large onions
225 g/8 oz French beans
50 g/2 oz butter
bay leaf

3 sprigs parsley
2 sprigs thyme
sprig of sage
pared rind of ½ lemon
salt and freshly ground black pepper
900 ml/1½ pints dry cider or chicken stock

Trim off the ends of the wings and legs from the chicken. Cut the carrots into chunks and cut the potatoes in half, or quarters if they are very large. Slice the onions fairly thickly and separate the slices into rings. Trim the French beans if they are fresh. Melt the butter in the wok and add the chicken. Fry, turning frequently, until well browned all over. Add the onion rings and cook for a few minutes. While the chicken is browning tie the bay leaf and the other herbs into a small bunch with the lemon rind.

Sprinkle a little seasoning over the chicken – add this sparingly at this stage if you are going to use ready-seasoned stock. Add the bouquet garni and pour in the cider or stock. Bring to the boil and put the lid on the wok. Reduce the heat so that the liquid simmers steadily and cook for 30 minutes. Open the wok and add the carrots and potatoes, then bring the liquid back to the boil, regulate the heat so that it simmers again and put the lid back on the wok. Simmer for a further 30 minutes. Add the French beans and cook for 10 minutes, then serve straight from the wok. SERVES 4

# Chicken Pudding

*If you don't happen to own a large saucepan and a steamer, then you will find that the wok is ideal for steaming traditional dishes like puddings. However, since you cannot pour a great depth of water into the wok, it is best to avoid those dishes which will take several hours to cook, or to cook the filling for the pudding first. This chicken pudding is warming and satisfying for a cold winter day.*

| | |
|---|---|
| 350 g/12 oz boneless chicken breast | 1 tablespoon plain flour |
| 25 g/1 oz butter | 150 ml/$\frac{1}{4}$ pint chicken stock |
| salt and freshly ground black pepper | 100 g/4 oz button mushrooms |
| | SUET PASTRY |
| generous pinch of dried thyme | 175 g/6 oz self-raising flour |
| 2 tablespoons chopped parsley | 75 g/3 oz shredded beef suet |
| bay leaf | salt |
| | about 150 ml/$\frac{1}{4}$ pint cold water |

Cut the chicken breast into small slices. Melt the butter in the wok, add the chicken and salt and pepper to taste, then fry until lightly browned on both sides. Stir in the herbs and flour and pour in the stock. Bring to the boil, then remove the meat and sauce from the wok and set aside to cool. Slice the mushrooms and stir them into the cooling chicken mixture.

To make the pastry, sift the flour into a bowl and stir in the suet with a pinch of salt. Add the water, mixing it in with a round-bladed knife to form a soft dough. Lightly knead the dough on a floured surface, then cut off about a third of it and set this aside for the lid. Roll out the remaining dough into a circle large enough to line a 900-ml/1$\frac{1}{2}$-pint pudding basin. Lightly butter the basin and lower the dough into it, making sure that the edges of the pastry stay on the rim of the basin. Press the pastry into the basin, making sure that no holes appear.

Put the cooled chicken filling into the basin, pressing it well down. Roll out the reserved pastry to make a lid and put it on top of the pudding filling. Brush the edges of the lid with water and fold the edges of the pastry which lines the basin over the top. Press down well to seal, then cover the top of the pudding with a piece of buttered greaseproof paper.

Wrap the whole of the pudding and the basin in foil, folding the edges very firmly so that no steam will enter during cooking. Stand the pudding on the steaming rack and pour in enough water to come up to the level of the basin. Bring to the boil and put the lid on the wok, then boil steadily for 45 minutes. Check to make sure that the water does not evaporate completely during cooking and top up with extra boiling water if necessary. Serve immediately. SERVES 4

# Chicken in High Spirits

*Save this recipe for special occasions and serve it with boiled rice flavoured with chopped tarragon and moistened with plenty of melted butter. A salad of lightly cooked French beans with chopped spring onions and watercress would go very well.*

4 boneless chicken breasts
4 tablespoons plain flour
salt and freshly ground black pepper
225 g/8 oz small button mushrooms
50 g/2 oz butter
300 ml/½ pint dry white wine
1 (396-g/14-oz) can artichoke hearts
2 tablespoons chopped chives
6 tablespoons brandy
150 ml/¼ pint soured cream to serve

Coat the chicken breasts with flour and plenty of seasoning. Cut the mushrooms in half and set aside.

Melt the butter in the wok and add the chicken breasts, then cook until golden brown on both sides. Sprinkle in any remaining flour and stir this into the butter. Pour in the wine and bring to the boil. Cover the wok and reduce the heat, then simmer for 15 minutes.

Drain the artichoke hearts and add them to the wok at the end of the cooking time. Stir into the sauce with the mushrooms and chives and cook for a minute.

It is best to serve this dish straight from the wok. Warm the brandy and pour it over the chicken, then ignite it immediately, before it has had time to mix with the sauce or lose its alcohol. Serve while still flaming, with a bowl of soured cream to spoon over the rich chicken and its sauce. SERVES 4

# Provençal Chicken

*Illustrated on page 49*

*Serve this simple chicken casserole with boiled or sautéed potatoes, buttered rice or pasta and a salad of mixed green vegetables.*

450 g/1 lb tomatoes
50 g/2 oz black olives
3 tablespoons plain flour
salt and freshly ground black pepper
4 chicken joints

3 tablespoons olive oil
2 large cloves garlic
bay leaf
150 ml/$\frac{1}{4}$ pint full-bodied red wine
chopped parsley to garnish

Place the tomatoes in a large bowl and cover with boiling water. Allow them to stand for 30 seconds to a minute, then drain and peel them. Cut the peeled tomatoes into quarters and set aside. Stone the olives and mix them with the tomatoes. Mix the flour with plenty of seasoning and use to coat the chicken joints.

Heat the oil in the wok and crush the garlic into it. Add the chicken joints and fry, turning frequently, until well browned on all sides. Add the bay leaf and pour in the wine, then spoon the tomatoes and olives over the top and bring just to boiling point. Put the lid on the wok and allow the chicken to simmer for 30 to 40 minutes. Sprinkle the parsley over before serving either straight from the wok or transferred to a warmed serving dish. SERVES 4

## Variations

Both lamb and pork taste excellent cooked in a provençal sauce. Substitute lamb cutlets (allowing two per person) or lean pork chops for the chicken in the above recipe. Reduce the amount of oil to 1 tablespoon if using pork.

# Two-flavoured Chicken

*Chicken steamed in the oriental way is absolutely mouth-watering! It bears no resemblance whatsoever to the pallid, tasteless steamed chicken we think of as food only for an invalid. Serve Simple Chop Suey (page 116) and some steamed rice as accompaniments.*

1 (1-kg/2-lb) oven-ready chicken
6 medium-thick slices fresh root ginger
4 tablespoons light soy sauce
small pinch of turmeric
4 tablespoons dry sherry
pared rind of 1 lemon

1 teaspoon cornflour
2 teaspoons water
GARNISH
a few spring onions
$\frac{1}{2}$ small red pepper
1 small lemon

Using a meat cleaver or a sharp knife and kitchen scissors, cut the chicken in half down its length. Pull off and discard all the skin and place the bird in a heatproof bowl or dish. A bowl with sloping sides is ideal as this allows room for the chicken, as well as being deep enough to accommodate the sauce. Remember to make sure that the dish will fit into the wok.

Arrange the slices of ginger on and around the chicken and sprinkle the soy sauce, turmeric and sherry over the top. Cut the lemon rind into very fine strips and sprinkle these over the chicken. Place the dish on the steaming rack in the wok and pour in enough water to come up as far as the base of the dish. Put the lid on the wok and bring the water to the boil, then steam steadily for 1 to $1\frac{1}{4}$ hours. About 20 minutes before the end of the cooking time mix the cornflour with the water and stir this carefully into the sauce

which surrounds the chicken. Continue cooking; the sauce is only very slightly thickened, so it will not become too thick during the remainder of the cooking time.

While the chicken cooks prepare the garnish. Some oriental dishes are highly decorated and this is one which can look very attractive with a colourful garnish but not quite as interesting without it. Trim the spring onions, snip and curl them (see Meatballs with Prawns, page 86); cut the red pepper into very fine strips and thinly slice the lemon. Cut the lemon slices in half if they are quite large.

Transfer the cooked chicken to a heated serving dish, discarding the slices of ginger. Pour the sauce over the chicken – if there is too much sauce for the serving dish, then serve some separately in a small heated bowl or sauceboat. Arrange the garnishing ingredients on and around the chicken and serve immediately. SERVES 4

# Chicken with Broccoli

*Illustrated on page 49*

*Here is a light and summery stir-fry dish which is not oriental. Serve it with boiled new potatoes sprinkled with chopped fresh herbs, or with boiled rice.*

450 g/1 lb boneless chicken breast
450 g/1 lb broccoli
50 g/2 oz butter
salt and freshly ground black pepper

50 g/2 oz flaked almonds
1 tablespoon plain flour
juice of 1 orange
150 ml/$\frac{1}{4}$ pint dry white wine

Cut the chicken meat into fine strips. Break the broccoli into small florets, cutting through the stalk if necessary and discarding any particularly tough stalks. Melt the butter in the wok and add the chicken strips. Season to taste and cook until they are browned all over, then stir in the almonds and cook until they are also lightly browned.

Sprinkle the flour over the chicken and stir over the heat for a minute. Pour in the orange juice and wine and bring to the boil, then reduce the heat and add the broccoli. Simmer for 2 minutes, or until the broccoli is just tender but still crisp and whole. Taste and adjust the seasoning if necessary and serve immediately. SERVES 4

# Kashmiri Chicken

*Illustrated on page 50*

*This is a richly spiced chicken curry, flavoured and thickened with ground fennel seeds and enriched with ghee, yogurt and cream – it's quite delicious! Serve plain boiled rice and some Indian bread as accompaniments. If you are going to serve Indian bread with this dish, for example parathas or naans (pages 150 and 151), prepare and roll out the bread in advance and set it aside, covered, until the chicken is ready. Transfer the chicken to a heated serving dish and keep it hot, then quickly wipe out the wok and grease it with oil ready to cook the bread.*

2 tablespoons fennel seeds
3 teaspoons ground ginger
6 green cardamoms
1 stick cinnamon
bay leaf
75 g/3 oz ghee (page 113)
50 g/2 oz flaked almonds

4 large chicken joints
salt
4 tablespoons concentrated tomato purée
300 ml/$\frac{1}{2}$ pint water
300 ml/$\frac{1}{2}$ pint natural yogurt

Grind the fennel seeds with the ginger, cardamoms, broken cinnamon stick and bay leaf to give a fine powder.

Melt the ghee in the wok, add the almonds and cook until golden brown. Then remove them with a slotted spoon and drain them on absorbent kitchen paper. Add the chicken joints to the ghee in the wok and cook until browned all over. Sprinkle over the ground spices and salt to taste, put the lid on the wok, then reduce the heat and allow the chicken to cook for 25 minutes. Open the wok and turn the chicken occasionally during cooking.

Dissolve the tomato purée in the water and add this to the wok. Bring the liquid to the boil and re-cover the wok, then reduce the heat and simmer for 30 minutes. Stir in the yogurt and continue to simmer for a further 15 minutes in the open wok. Sprinkle the fried almonds over and serve, straight from the wok. SERVES 4

*Top:* Turkey in the Grass (page 67); *bottom:* Peanut-coated Turkey (page 66)

# Crispy Chicken Wun Tuns

*These crunchy, chicken-filled wun tuns are incredibly scrumptious and, although rather time-consuming to make, well worth the effort.*
*Serve them as an interesting first course or as part of a spread of Chinese food.*

2 small boneless chicken breasts
2 tablespoons soy sauce
1 clove garlic
pinch of five spice powder (page 42)
1 quantity wun tun dough (page 94)

1 egg, beaten
900 ml/1½ pints oil for deep frying
GARNISH
a few spring onion curls (see Meatballs with Prawns, page 86)
1 lemon, cut into wedges

Cut each chicken breast into nine small pieces. The pieces should only be about the size of a small thumb nail so don't choose large chicken breasts. Place the chicken pieces in a basin and pour over the soy sauce. Crush the garlic into the basin and sprinkle the five spice powder in. Stir well to coat all the chicken pieces in the seasonings, then cover and leave to marinate for several hours – overnight is best.

Prepare the wun tun dough according to the recipe instructions, or use bought wun tun skins. Roll out the dough as explained in the recipe for Pork Wun Tuns and place a piece of chicken in the middle of each square. Brush round the edge of the chicken with a little beaten egg, then gather up the dough to enclose the meat completely, sealing it in well but leaving the edges of the dough free. The filled wun tuns should look like small gathered muslin herb bags.

Heat the oil for deep frying in the wok to 190 C/375 F and add the wun tuns, a few at a time. Fry until crisp and golden, then drain on absorbent kitchen paper and arrange on a warmed serving platter. Garnish with spring onion curls and lemon wedges before serving. SERVES 4

*Top:* Oriental Duck with Pineapple (page 72); *bottom:* Wun Tun Duck (page 71)

# Sweet and Sour Chicken

*The sweet and sour sauce which accompanies the crisp-fried chicken in this recipe is also delicious with other meats and fish. It can be served with crisp, batter-coated pork pieces or prawns, with pork spare ribs or with lamb chops. Serve the chicken with steamed rice and crisp fried noodles.*

| | |
|---|---|
| 1 large green pepper | 2 tablespoons dry sherry |
| 1 large onion | 1 teaspoon cornflour |
| 3 carrots | 2 teaspoons water |
| 1 stick celery | 4 chicken joints |
| 3 canned pineapple rings | 2 tablespoons plain flour |
| 2 tablespoons soy sauce | salt and freshly ground black |
| 2 tablespoons cider vinegar | pepper |
| 2 tablespoons dark brown sugar | 2 tablespoons oil |
| 2 tablespoons concentrated tomato purée | |

Cut the stalk end off the green pepper, scoop out and discard all the seeds and pith, and cut the flesh into thin slices. Slice the onion, then separate the slices into rings. Cut the carrots and celery into fine strips, and cut the pineapple rings into small pieces.

In a measuring jug, mix the soy sauce, vinegar, sugar, tomato purée and sherry, then make the mixture up to 250 ml/8 fl oz with water. Stir well to dissolve the sugar. Mix the cornflour with the water and stir this into the liquid ingredients. Set aside.

Coat the chicken joints in the flour and sprinkle a little seasoning over them. Heat the oil in the wok, add the chicken and fry it over a medium heat, turning occasionally, until well browned on all sides. By this time the joints should be cooked through; to test if they are ready, pierce the thickest part of the joint with a pointed knife – the juices should be clear with no sign of blood. If you are in any doubt as to whether the chicken is cooked, then continue frying the joints over a low to medium heat without letting them become too brown. Remove the chicken pieces from the wok and drain them on absorbent kitchen paper. Set aside and keep hot.

To make the sauce, add the pepper, onion, carrot and celery to the fat left in the wok and stir-fry for 2 minutes. First stir the liquid ingredients in the jug, as they may have separated on standing, then pour the sauce over the vegetables in the wok. Cook, stirring, over a high heat until the sauce boils, then simmer for a minute. Stir in the pineapple and spoon the sauce over the chicken in a warmed serving dish. Alternatively, the chicken can be returned to the wok for serving. SERVES 4

# Variations

**Sweet and Sour Pork**
Mix 100 g/4 oz self-raising flour with 150 ml/$\frac{1}{4}$ pint cold water to make a smooth batter, beating well to remove lumps. Trim 450 g/1 lb lean pork and cut it into small cubes. Now prepare the sauce in the wok as above, adding a little oil for frying first, transfer it to a warmed serving dish and keep hot. Quickly rinse and wipe out the wok. Pour in 900 ml/1$\frac{1}{2}$ pints oil and heat it to 190 C/360 F. Whisk 1 egg white until it stands in stiff peaks, then fold it into the batter. Dip the pieces of pork in the batter, then cook them in the hot oil until crisp and golden. Drain on absorbent kitchen paper and serve immediately, with the sauce.

**Sweet and Sour Spare Ribs**
Simmer 675 g/1$\frac{1}{2}$ lb pork spare ribs in water to cover, with a little salt, for 30 minutes. Drain, wipe out the wok and fry the ribs in 2 tablespoons oil until golden brown. Transfer to a heated serving dish and prepare the sauce as above. Serve immediately.

# Chick Pea Chicken

*Nutty-flavoured chick peas complement the chicken perfectly in this dish which can be served with just a green salad to make a light meal.*

| | |
|---|---|
| 1 onion | salt and freshly ground black |
| 4 chicken joints | pepper |
| 50 g/2 oz black olives | 2 cloves garlic |
| 3 tablespoons olive oil | 2 (439-g/15$\frac{1}{2}$-oz) cans chick peas |
| | 2 tablespoons chopped fresh herbs |

Chop the onion. Trim the chicken joints of any excess skin or fat and cut off the very ends of their wings or legs. Stone the olives. Heat the oil in the wok, season the chicken joints and add them to the wok with the onion. Crush the garlic over the chicken and fry over medium heat, turning the pieces over once, until they are golden brown all over – this should take about 15 minutes to give the chicken time to start cooking through.

Add the drained chick peas to the wok and sprinkle the olives over, then put the lid on and reduce the heat so that the food simmers away in its own juice. Cook for about 30 minutes. Turn the chicken joints once during this cooking time and make sure that they are cooked through by piercing them at the thickest part: if they are cooked the juices will be free of any blood. Sprinkle the fresh herbs over the chicken and serve immediately. SERVES 4

# Peanut-coated Turkey

*Illustrated on page 61*

*These nutty turkey fillets are quick to prepare and cook, so they can be fried in the wok after the vegetable accompaniment has been finished. For example, why not try serving them with Cabbage Braise (page 106) or Creamed Mushrooms and Potatoes (page 108)?*

| | |
|---|---|
| 225 g/8 oz salted peanuts | 1 tablespoon oil |
| freshly ground black pepper | GARNISH |
| 4 large turkey fillets | 4 tomatoes |
| 4 tablespoons plain flour | 1 small onion |
| 1 egg, lightly beaten | chopped parsley |

Finely chop the peanuts and season them with a little pepper, then place them on a plate. Dip the turkey fillets first in the flour, then in the beaten egg, and finally in the nuts, pressing them on well.

Heat the oil in the wok, add the turkey fillets and cook, turning once, until golden on both sides and cooked through. Transfer to a heated serving dish and keep hot. Slice the tomatoes and onion and separate the onion slices into rings. Arrange these on top of the turkey fillets and sprinkle the parsley in a neat row down the middle; serve immediately. SERVES 4

# Turkey in the Grass

*Illustrated on page 61*

*This is a delicious dish with a very silly title – in fact it should be called 'grass in the turkey' but that sounds particularly unappetising! However, there is grass in the recipe: lemon grass is used to give simple stir-fried turkey flavour and an excellent aroma. Serve with a rice dish.*

675 g/1½ lb boneless turkey breast
3 thick stalks lemon grass
25 g/1 oz fresh root ginger
50 g/2 oz butter
1 clove garlic

1 tablespoon rich soy sauce
1 head curly endive
3 spring onions
1 lemon, cut into wedges, to garnish

Cut the turkey into bite-sized cubes. Cut the lemon grass in half lengthways and then cut the strips in half widthways. Slice the ginger and mix it with the lemon grass.

Melt the butter in the wok, crush the garlic into it and add the lemon grass and ginger. Cook, stirring continuously, for a few minutes, then add the turkey and continue stir-frying until the meat has browned all over and is cooked through. Add the soy sauce and cook gently for a few minutes more.

Separate and rinse the leaves of endive, dry them thoroughly, then arrange them on a serving dish. Trim and chop the spring onions and sprinkle them over the endive. Arrange the turkey on top and pour over any juices from the wok. Serve immediately, garnished with the lemon wedges – when served, the juice can be squeezed from these to add zest to the turkey and salad. SERVES 4

# Braised Turkey Joint

*I was really pleased when this recipe worked – it is so useful being able to cook a large piece of meat without turning the oven on, and without having to stew it in gallons of sauce. If you have limited kitchen facilities, and an oven doesn't form part of them, you will find your wok invaluable for cooking whole chickens, joints of turkey or those pre-packed bacon joints that don't have to be boiled in lots of water.*

1 (1-kg/2¼-lb) turkey joint
4 large potatoes
450 g/1 lb carrots
oil
450 g/1 lb pickling onions
salt and freshly ground black pepper

2 bay leaves
a few sprigs of fresh herbs (for example, thyme, sage and parsley)
150 ml/¼ pint dry white wine or stock

Take the wrapping off the joint; it is best to choose one which has a plastic wrapping rather than one which has a string coat which is meant to be cooked on the joint to hold it together.

Cut each of the potatoes into a few thick slices, then cut the carrots into fairly thick slices. Heat a little oil in the wok and add the onions. Cook them for a few minutes, then remove them from the pan with a slotted spoon. Add the joint and brown it on all sides until golden. Add the prepared vegetables and onions, arranging them round the turkey and sprinkling plenty of seasoning over them. Put the bay leaves and herbs on top and pour in the wine or stock. Bring to the boil, then reduce the heat to a very low setting so that the liquid barely simmers. Put the lid on the wok and cook very slowly for 1¼ to 1½ hours, or until the turkey is cooked through to the middle. I found that it was cooked after 1¼ hours but this will vary slightly with the joint.

Remove the joint to a serving platter and surround it with the cooked vegetables. If you like you can add more wine or stock to the pan juices, boil them up and thicken slightly with a mixture of 1 tablespoon plain flour creamed with 25 g/1 oz butter. Small knobs of this mixture should be whisked into the sauce and boiled for a minute to thicken it. SERVES 4 to 6

## Variations

You can vary this dish simply by adding other vegetables and spices. For example, red and green peppers can be sliced and added with herbs like oregano or marjoram, or with tomatoes and garlic. Dried fruits, such as apricots, can be roughly chopped and added along with some sliced celery. Even cored and peeled whole apples can be cooked in the wok with the meat, to give an apple sauce when ready to serve.

# Fruited Turkey
# with Bread Dumplings

*Serve this delicious turkey casserole as a main meal with the satisfying dumplings, and perhaps a green salad with a few segments of orange as an accompaniment. You can, if you like, omit the dumplings and serve the turkey on a bed of cooked rice or pasta.*

1 kg/2 lb boneless turkey breast
25 g/1 oz butter
1 clove garlic
salt and freshly ground black pepper
1 tablespoon plain flour
1 (428-g/15-oz) can apricot halves in syrup
300 ml/$\frac{1}{2}$ pint dry cider
1 teaspoon whole grain mustard
1 tablespoon capers
chopped fresh parsley to garnish

DUMPLINGS
100 g/4 oz very fine dry breadcrumbs (made from stale bread, either white or brown)
50 g/2 oz self-raising flour
$\frac{1}{2}$ teaspoon dried thyme
$\frac{1}{2}$ teaspoon caraway seeds
50 g/2 oz butter
salt and freshly ground black pepper
200–250 ml/6–8 fl oz milk

Cut the turkey into cubes. Melt the butter in the wok and add the turkey cubes, then crush the garlic into the pan and sprinkle over seasoning to taste. Fry until the turkey cubes are well browned on all sides, then stir in the flour and cook for a minute before pouring in the apricot halves with their syrup and the cider. Bring to the boil, stirring, then add the mustard and capers. Reduce the heat so that the casserole barely simmers while you make the dumplings.

Mix the breadcrumbs with the flour, thyme and caraway seeds and rub in the butter until the mixture is once again very fine in texture. Add seasoning and pour in sufficient milk to make a stiff dough. Shape the mixture into eight to ten dumplings about the size of small eggs.

Bring the turkey casserole back to boiling point, then reduce the heat so that it simmers gently. Place the dumplings on the surface of the casserole and put the lid on the wok, then simmer gently for 20 minutes. Serve immediately, sprinkled with plenty of parsley to garnish. SERVES 4

# Duck with Apricots

*This is a rich casserole for special occasion dinners – serve it with new or sautéed potatoes, buttered pasta shapes or boiled rice flavoured with a little grated orange rind and a pinch of ground cinnamon.*

4 duck joints
1 onion
oil
salt and freshly ground black pepper
2 sprigs rosemary

100 g/4 oz dried apricots
900 ml/1½ pints full-bodied red wine
a few extra sprigs of rosemary to garnish

Trim any excess fat off the duck joints and thinly slice the onion. Grease the wok with a little oil and add the duck joints, then fry them all over until really well browned. You will find that they give up a lot of fat during this initial cooking. Remove the duck joints from the wok and drain them on absorbent kitchen paper. Drain all but a thin coating of fat from the wok.

Add the onion to the wok and fry until soft but not browned. Season to taste and add the rosemary. Return the duck joints to the wok and add the apricots, then pour in the wine and bring to the boil. Reduce the heat and put the lid on the wok, then simmer for an hour, or until the duck is tender.

Taste and adjust the seasoning if necessary, then arrange the duck joints on a serving platter and spoon the sauce neatly over and around them. Garnish with a few extra sprigs of fresh rosemary and serve immediately.
SERVES 4

# Variations

**Cherry Duck**
Omit the rosemary from the above recipe and substitute 450 g/1 lb black cherries for the apricots. Remove the stones from the cherries and add them to the duck 15 minutes before the end of the cooking time.

**Duck in Orange Sauce**
Omit the rosemary and apricots from the above recipe. Grate the rind from two oranges and squeeze the juice from three. Sprinkle the rind over the fried and drained duck portions and pour in the juice. Substitute half white wine and half chicken stock for the red wine and continue to cook as above. Thicken the sauce by whisking in a knob of beurre manié 5 minutes before the end of the cooking time. (To make beurre manié beat 1 tablespoon plain flour into 50 g/2 oz butter until smooth.)

# Wun Tun Duck

*Illustrated on page 62*

*You can either make the wun tuns yourself or you can buy the skins from a Chinese supermarket. The combination of cooked duck, crisp wun tuns and the sweet and sour sauce in this recipe is well worth all the effort. If you intend to serve this for a dinner party, cook the duck and prepare the wun tun dough in advance.*

1 oven-ready duck
1.15 litres/2 pints water
4–5 tablespoons soy sauce
4 slices fresh root ginger
1 quantity wun tun dough (page 94)
1 red pepper
1 carrot

1 small onion
1 tablespoon oil
2 tablespoons tomato ketchup
2 tablespoons cider vinegar
2 tablespoons dry sherry
1 tablespoon sugar
900 ml/1½ pints oil for deep frying

Trim off the ends of the wings and legs of the duck and cut the duck in half lengthways. Place both pieces of duck in the wok and pour in the water. Add 3 tablespoons of the soy sauce and the ginger and bring to the boil. Reduce the heat so that the liquid simmers steadily and put the lid on the wok. Cook for an hour, checking occasionally that the water has not dried up and turning the duck half-way through the cooking time.

Prepare the wun tun dough and roll it out according to the recipe instructions. Keep it covered while preparing the sauce. Cut the stalk end off the red pepper and remove all the seeds and pith from inside, then halve and thinly slice the flesh. Cut the carrot into very fine strips and halve and thinly slice the onion, separating the pieces into fine strips.

When the duck is cooked, remove it from the wok and drain thoroughly. Leave until cool enough to handle, then cut off all the meat. Discard any fat and cut the meat into strips. Pour off the stock, reserving it for use in soups and stews. Rinse and wipe out the wok, greasing it if necessary.

Add the oil to the wok and heat over a high heat. Fry the strips of duck until browned, then add the pepper, carrot and onion strips and cook quickly over a high heat. Stir in the ketchup, vinegar, sherry, remaining soy sauce and the sugar and bring to the boil. Transfer to a dish and keep hot.

To cook the wun tuns, wipe out the wok and add the oil for deep frying. Heat to 190 C/375 F and add the squares of wun tun dough, a few at a time, cooking them until crisp and golden brown. Place them on a heated serving platter and spoon the duck with sauce into the centre. Serve immediately.
SERVES 4

# Oriental Duck with Pineapple

*Illustrated on page 62*

*When I tested this recipe I jotted down 'delicious' and 'amazing' at the end of my notes, because the combination of simmering and frying makes the duck meat both tender and well flavoured. You can use canned pineapple in natural juice instead of the fresh fruit in this recipe, but the end result warrants buying a fresh pineapple. Served with steamed or boiled rice, this dish makes a complete meal – serve it straight from the wok and offer chopsticks and small bowls as the only eating implements.*

1 oven-ready duck
1.15 litres/2 pints water
3 tablespoons rich soy sauce
1 fresh pineapple
1 (227-g/8-oz) can water chestnuts

1 bunch spring onions
2 green chillies
sesame oil
1 large clove garlic

Cut the duck in half lengthways, using a meat cleaver and poultry scissors. Place the halves in the wok and pour in the water, then add 1 tablespoon of the soy sauce. Put the lid on the wok and bring to the boil. Reduce the heat so that the liquid simmers steadily and cook for an hour.

While the duck is cooking prepare the remaining ingredients. Trim the leaves off the pineapple and cut off the stalk end. Cut off the peel and cut out all the spines, then slice the fruit in half lengthways and remove the hard core. Cut the pineapple halves into slices and set aside. Drain and slice the water chestnuts and slice the spring onions diagonally. Cut the stalks off the chillies and remove all their seeds, then slice the green part thinly.

At the end of the simmering time remove the duck from the stock and set it aside. Pour the stock out of the wok (this should be chilled and the fat skimmed off, then the stock can be used in oriental soups and stews) and wipe out the pan. Grease it with a little sesame oil.

When the duck is cool enough to handle cut all the meat off the bones and slice it into pieces. Heat the wok and add the chillies, crush the garlic into the pan and add the duck. Stir-fry until lightly browned, then add the water chestnuts and pineapple and cook for a few minutes. Stir in the remaining soy sauce and any juice from the fruit, and sprinkle over the spring onions. Cook for a minute before serving straight from the wok. SERVES 4

# Meat Dishes

*Amongst these recipes there is a dish for every occasion – a homely pork casserole with dumplings served straight from the wok for a satisfying meal, mouth-watering spare ribs in barbecue sauce, heart-warming chilli con carne to share with friends, or more formal veal recipes which are ideal for dinner party menus.*

*When time is short, liven up a few simple chops with some of the ideas from this chapter, and for those times when you really feel like cooking, why not prepare a Chinese feast? Make some delicious wun tuns or a selection of dishes with pork and beef. Or, if you're in the mood for a little spice, try your hand at some Indian dishes; they're all here for the making. Variety is the spice of life, they say, and there is certainly plenty of that in this collection of meaty meals!*

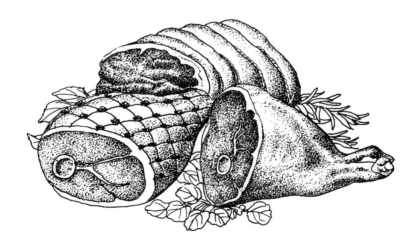

# Beef Stroganoff

*This is incredibly quick to cook and ideal both for cooking in, and serving straight from, the wok. Serve with buttered rice or pasta and a fresh green salad.*

1 kg/2 lb frying steak
1 onion
100 g/4 oz button mushrooms
50 g/2 oz butter

salt and freshly ground black pepper
4 tablespoons brandy
150 ml/$\frac{1}{4}$ pint soured cream
chopped parsley to garnish

Cut the steak into fine strips. Halve the onion and slice it very thinly, then separate the pieces into fine strips. Slice the mushrooms thinly.

Melt the butter in the wok and add the onion strips and seasoning to taste, then fry until softened. Turn up the heat and make sure that the butter is as hot as it can be without burning, then add the meat and cook very quickly until browned. Stir all the time as the meat cooks to prevent it sticking to the wok. Pour the brandy over the beef and ignite it straightaway. Stir in the mushrooms and heat for a minute, then streak the soured cream through the meat and sprinkle with a little chopped parsley. Serve immediately. SERVES 4

## Variations

The stroganoff can be made at less cost using fine strips of lean pork. Lamb is also delicious cooked in this way — choose lean boneless meat from the leg and cut it into fine strips as above.

# Meatball Hotpot

*Illustrated on page 79*

*This is a flavoursome, satisfying one-pot meal for winter days. Serve plenty of crusty bread and butter and a great wedge of mature Cheddar or Stilton cheese to complete the meal.*

675 g/1½ lb lean minced beef
50 g/2 oz fresh breadcrumbs
salt and freshly ground black pepper
4 tablespoons chopped parsley
2 cloves garlic
dash of Worcestershire sauce
1 large egg, lightly beaten
225 g/8 oz carrots
1 kg/2 lb potatoes
½ small swede

450 g/1 lb pickling onions
100 g/4 oz button mushrooms
2 tablespoons oil
2 tablespoons plain flour
300 ml/½ pint beef stock
600 ml/1 pint brown ale
4 tablespoons concentrated tomato purée
bay leaf
chopped parsley to garnish

Place the mince in a bowl with the breadcrumbs, then add plenty of seasoning, the parsley, crushed garlic and Worcestershire sauce. Mix thoroughly and stir in the beaten egg to bind all the ingredients. Take spoonfuls of the meat mixture and, using the palms of your hands, shape the mixture into meatballs about the size of a small egg.

Slice the carrots thickly, cut the potatoes and swede into chunks, and trim the pickling onions or cut them in half if they are very large. Trim the ends of the mushroom stalks.

Heat the oil in the wok and add the meatballs, frying them until brown on all sides. Take care when turning the meatballs that you do not break them up. Remove from the pan with a slotted spoon and set aside. Add the carrots, potatoes, swede and onions to the wok and fry for a few minutes, stirring the vegetables all the time. Sprinkle the flour over the vegetables and stir for a minute, then pour in the stock and ale and bring to the boil. Add the tomato purée and bay leaf, stir well, then return the meatballs to the wok and put on the lid. Reduce the heat so that the hotpot simmers steadily and cook for 45 to 50 minutes, or until all the vegetables are tender; do not allow the sauce to cook too rapidly or it may break up the meatballs. Add the mushrooms after about 30 minutes' cooking time – no sooner or they will be overcooked.

Serve the hotpot straight from the wok, sprinkled with a little more chopped parsley to garnish. SERVES 4

# Devilled Beef Fritters

*These light meaty fritters are absolutely delicious; they are spicy and well seasoned, and they are complemented by a simple dressing of yogurt and paprika. Serve warm pita bread with the fritters.*

450 g/1 lb lean minced beef or
minced steak
2 tablespoons tomato ketchup
2 teaspoons Dijon mustard
dash of Worcestershire sauce
2 cloves garlic
salt and freshly ground black
pepper
$\frac{1}{2}$ teaspoon paprika
8 tablespoons self-raising flour
4 eggs

4 tablespoons natural yogurt
1 red pepper
1 green pepper
1 small onion
1 crisp lettuce (cos or iceberg) *or* 2
lettuce hearts
oil for frying
SAUCE
300 ml/$\frac{1}{2}$ pint natural yogurt
paprika

Place the mince in a basin and mix in the ketchup, mustard and Worcestershire sauce. Crush the garlic over the meat and mix this in with plenty of salt and pepper and the paprika. Sprinkle the flour, a tablespoon at a time, over the meat mixture and mix in each spoonful so that it is thoroughly and smoothly incorporated. Lightly beat the eggs and pour them over the meat mixture. Gradually mix them in and beat well, then pour in the yogurt and beat the batter thoroughly.

Cut the stalk ends off the peppers and remove all the seeds and pith from inside. Cut the pepper flesh into fine slices. Thinly slice the onion and separate the slices into rings. Separate the lettuce leaves and shred them coarsely.

Heat a little oil in the wok and drop spoonfuls of the batter on to the hot surface – several fritters can be cooked at once on the lower part of the sides of the wok. The fritters should be fairly small, so use large teaspoonfuls of the mixture, or small tablespoonfuls. Cook the fritters until they are thoroughly browned on both sides, then transfer them to absorbent kitchen paper, drain and keep hot. Repeat until all the batter is used.

Add the onion rings and pepper slices to the fat remaining in the pan and stir-fry these for a minute or two, until the onion is just beginning to soften. Arrange the lettuce on a large serving platter and top with the onion and pepper mixture. Arrange the fritters on top and serve, with a bowl of natural yogurt topped with a little paprika. SERVES 4

# Variations

**Spiced Lamb Fritters**
Substitute lean minced lamb for the beef, omit the tomato ketchup and add 2 teaspoons of ground coriander to the batter. Serve the cooked fritters with a bowl of natural yogurt, sprinkled liberally with chopped fresh coriander leaves.
**Chilli Pork Fritters** (*Illustrated on page 80*)
Substitute lean minced pork for the beef and omit the ketchup, mustard and Worcestershire sauce. Add 4 finely chopped green chillies to the meat batter and stir in the grated rind of $\frac{1}{2}$ orange. Cook and serve as in the main recipe on the left.

# Chilli con Carne

*This is a quick version of an old favourite, made using canned kidney beans. Serve the chilli straight from the wok, with plenty of boiled rice and a crisp green salad.*

1 large onion
2 large red peppers
2 tablespoons oil
2 cloves garlic
675 g/1½ lb lean minced beef
salt and freshly ground black pepper

2 tablespoons plain flour
1–2 tablespoons chilli powder
600 ml/1 pint beef stock
4 tablespoons concentrated tomato purée
2 (425-g/15-oz) cans red kidney beans

Finely slice the onion. Cut the stalk ends off the red peppers and remove all the seeds and pith from the inside. Cut the flesh into fine slices.

Heat the oil in the wok and crush the garlic into it, then add the onion and peppers and cook until softened. Remove from the pan with a slotted spoon, then add the minced beef and salt and pepper to taste to the oil remaining in the wok. Fry, breaking up the meat as it cooks, until well browned, then stir in the flour and chilli powder to taste and cook for a few minutes. Gradually pour in the stock and stir in the tomato purée, then bring to the boil. Return the onion and peppers to the pan and reduce the heat so that the meat simmers gently. Cook, covered, for about 45 minutes, or until the mince is very tender.

Drain the beans and stir them into the chilli, then cook, uncovered, for a further 5 minutes before serving. SERVES 4

# Italian Veal Olives

*Veal escalopes, stuffed with Dolcelatte, braised on courgettes and garnished with olives, make this dish ideal dinner party fare. Serve buttered pasta as the only accompaniment.*

4 veal escalopes
100 g/4 oz Dolcelatte cheese
2 tablespoons single cream
salt and freshly ground black pepper
1 tablespoon chopped fresh basil (optional)
4 small courgettes

2 spring onions
2 tablespoons olive oil
2 tablespoons plain flour
4 tablespoons dry white wine
GARNISH
100 g/4 oz black olives
2 tablespoons chopped parsley
2 tomatoes, chopped

Place the escalopes between two sheets of greaseproof paper and beat them out as thinly as possible. Mix the Dolcelatte with the cream, a little salt and freshly ground black pepper, and the basil, if used. Spread this mixture over the veal escalopes, then roll them up neatly to enclose the stuffing. Secure with wooden cocktail sticks and set aside in the refrigerator.

Trim off and discard the ends of the courgettes and cut the courgettes into slices. Chop the spring onions.

Heat the oil in the wok. Dust the veal rolls with the flour and brown them thoroughly in the hot oil, then, using a slotted spoon, remove them from the pan. Add the courgettes to the oil and toss them lightly, then add the spring onions and wine, and place the veal rolls on top. Cover the wok and simmer for 15 minutes. While the veal is cooking stone and chop the black olives for the garnish.

When cooked, the veal can be transferred to a suitable heated serving dish, with the courgettes arranged around the rolls, or, if your wok is attractive enough, the dish can be served straight from the pan. Sprinkle the black olives, parsley and tomatoes in neat rows to garnish the veal, then serve immediately. SERVES 4

**Right** Meatball Hotpot (page 75)
**Overleaf** *top:* Chilli Pork Fritters (page 77); *bottom:* Wiener Schnitzel (page 81)

# Wiener Schnitzel

*Illustrated on page 80*

*Serve this traditional dish of fried, breaded veal escalopes with sautéed potatoes and broccoli, French beans or a mixed salad.*

4 veal escalopes
3 tablespoons plain flour
salt and freshly ground black
pepper
1 egg, beaten
100 g/4 oz dry white breadcrumbs

75 g/3 oz butter
GARNISH
2 hard-boiled eggs, chopped
chopped parsley
1 lemon, sliced

Place the escalopes between two sheets of greaseproof paper and beat them out until they are very thin. Mix the flour with plenty of seasoning on a plate and dip the veal in it. Coat the escalopes first in beaten egg and then in the breadcrumbs, pressing them on well.

Melt the butter in the wok and add the veal. Fry until golden on the underside, turning round once so that the coating browns evenly, then turn over and brown the second side. Transfer the cooked veal escalopes to a heated serving platter, pour any pan juices over, and arrange a garnish of chopped hard-boiled egg and chopped parsley round them. Top with slices of lemon and serve immediately. SERVES 4

# Veal with Salami

*Illustrated on page 89*

*This dish is very rich – serve it with buttered pasta and a tomato salad. A cheaper and equally delicious version can be prepared with chicken instead.*

4 veal escalopes
225 g/8 oz Italian salami
225 g/8 oz black olives
1 tablespoon oil

4 tablespoons chopped chives
150 ml/$\frac{1}{4}$ pint soured cream
freshly ground black pepper
paprika to garnish (optional)

Cut the veal and the salami into fine strips and remove the stones from the olives. Heat the oil in the wok, add the veal strips and stir-fry until golden brown. Stir in the olives and salami strips and cook for a minute, then sprinkle over the chopped chives and drizzle the cream over but do not stir it in. Sprinkle with plenty of freshly ground black pepper – this dish should not need any salt because the salami is already highly seasoned – and serve immediately. Garnish with a little paprika, if you like. SERVES 4

# Lamb Biriani

*Birianis are spiced Indian dishes of meat or poultry, with rice cooked in the sauce. This lamb biriani is mild and spicy, and deliciously moist. Serve it with Fresh Mint Chutney (page 156), Tomato Sambal (below) and crisp papadums.*

| | |
|---|---|
| 1 kg/2 lb lean boneless lamb | 4 cloves garlic |
| 2 large onions | $\frac{1}{2}$ teaspoon turmeric |
| 50 g/2 oz fresh root ginger | salt and freshly ground black |
| 4 green cardamoms | pepper |
| 1 stick cinnamon | 600 ml/1 pint water |
| bay leaf | 2 tablespoons concentrated tomato |
| 2 cloves | purée |
| 50 g/2 oz ghee (page 113) | 225 g/8 oz long-grain rice |

Cut the lamb into large chunks. Finely chop the onions and grate the ginger. Grind the cardamoms, cinnamon, bay leaf and cloves together until they form a powder.

Melt the ghee in the wok and add the meat. Fry, turning frequently, until well browned on all sides. Remove the lamb from the pan and add the onion and ginger to the fat remaining in the wok. Crush the garlic into the pan and fry, stirring frequently, until the onion is soft but not browned. Add the ground spices and turmeric, with salt and pepper to taste, and cook for a few minutes before returning the meat to the wok. Stir well to coat the meat in the spice mixture, then pour in the water and stir in the tomato purée. Bring to the boil, reduce the heat and cover the wok, then simmer for 30 minutes.

Stir the rice into the wok and continue cooking for a further 30 minutes over a low heat. Check that the rice does not stick to the base of the wok during cooking and add a little more water if necessary. When cooked the biriani should not be completely dry, but it should be moist without an excess of sauce. Serve immediately, straight from the wok or from a heated serving dish. SERVES 4

### Tomato Sambal
Place 450 g/1 lb tomatoes in a bowl and cover with boiling water. Leave for 30 seconds to a minute, then drain, peel and chop finely. Place the chopped tomatoes in a small bowl. Mix together $\frac{1}{2}$ teaspoon each of chilli powder and sugar, the juice of $\frac{1}{2}$ lemon, plenty of seasoning and 2 tablespoons chopped coriander leaves. Mix this into the tomatoes. Finely chop one small onion and sprinkle over the top. Lightly chill before serving.

# Lamb with Aubergines

*This dish is quick to cook and delicious with a simple green salad and some boiled new potatoes. Alternatively, the lamb and vegetables can be served straight from the wok, with plenty of French bread offered as an accompaniment.*

8 lamb cutlets
2 large aubergines
salt and freshly ground black pepper
6 large tomatoes
olive oil for frying
2 cloves garlic

SAUCE
2 tablespoons chopped mint
150 ml/$\frac{1}{4}$ pint natural yogurt
freshly ground black pepper
GARNISH
1 lemon, sliced
sprigs of mint

Trim any excess fat from the lamb cutlets. Trim the ends off the aubergines and slice them fairly thickly. Place the aubergine slices in a colander and sprinkle a little salt over them. Set aside for 20 minutes. Meanwhile, place the tomatoes in a large bowl and pour in enough boiling water to cover them. Allow to stand for 30 seconds to a minute, then drain and peel them. Slice the tomatoes thickly and dry the aubergine slices.

Heat some olive oil in the wok and add the lamb cutlets. Cook over fairly high heat until browned on both sides and all round the edge. Continue cooking the cutlets, over a reduced heat, until they are cooked to your liking. Remove from the wok and drain on absorbent kitchen paper, then keep the cutlets hot while you prepare the vegetables.

Add a little more oil to the wok and fry the aubergine slices, with the garlic crushed over them, until they are lightly browned on both sides. You may have to add a little extra oil during cooking as the aubergines tend to absorb it. When all the slices are cooked, push them to one side and add the tomato slices. Cook these for just a few seconds, then sprinkle with seasoning and mix with the aubergines.

Prepare a yogurt mint sauce simply by stirring the mint into the yogurt and seasoning the mixture lightly with black pepper. Place this in a small serving bowl.

Return the cutlets to the wok, arranging them neatly on top of the vegetables. Garnish with lemon slices and sprigs of mint and serve immediately, with the sauce handed separately. SERVES 4

# Nargisi Kofta Curry

*This is a traditional Indian dish – I was most surprised when I first ordered it and found that concealed in the meatballs were hard-boiled eggs! In fact the spicy lamb coat perfectly complements the hidden eggs and the resulting curry is both delicious and substantial. Serve crisp papadums (grilled or fried), boiled or steamed rice and Cucumber Raita (below) as accompaniments.*

4 green chillies
1 large onion
2 cloves garlic
25 g/1 oz fresh root ginger
450 g/1 lb lean minced lamb
1 egg
2 tablespoons chick pea flour or plain flour
salt and freshly ground black pepper
8 hard-boiled eggs
plain flour for coating

50 g/2 oz ghee (page 113) *or* 2 tablespoons oil
large bay leaf
4 cloves
4 green cardamoms
1 stick cinnamon
2 tablespoons garam masala
1 (397-g/14-oz) can tomatoes
150 ml/$\frac{1}{4}$ pint natural yogurt
chopped fresh coriander leaves to garnish

Trim the stalk ends off the chillies, split them open and remove and discard all the seeds (these are very hot indeed), then chop the green flesh. Finely chop the onion and garlic and grate the root ginger; do not peel the ginger first – simply scrub the skin and grate the whole piece on a coarse grater. Discard any small piece of skin which remains when all the ginger has been grated.

Mix the lamb with half the chopped chillies, the garlic, raw egg and chick pea flour or ordinary flour. Add plenty of seasoning and mix all the ingredients thoroughly so that they bind together well. Divide the meat mixture in half and then divide each half into four. Shape one portion of the meat mixture into a round cake in the palm of your hand (wet your hands first so that the meat does not stick to them) and place a hard-boiled egg on top. Knead the meat evenly around the egg to cover it completely and form a neat ball. Coat the kofta with a little flour and set aside, then repeat the process with the remaining meat and eggs.

Melt the ghee or heat the oil in the wok, add the prepared kofta and fry them, turning carefully, until browned all over. Remove from the wok and set aside on absorbent kitchen paper. Add the bay leaf and whole spices to the fat remaining in the wok and stir-fry for a few minutes. Stir in the remaining chillies and the onion and ginger and cook until the onion is soft but not browned. Add the garam masala and stir-fry for a few minutes. Pour in the tomatoes and yogurt and heat to boiling point, then return the kofta to the wok and put the lid on. Simmer gently for 30 minutes, turning the kofta over half-way through cooking.

Serve hot, garnished with plenty of chopped coriander. SERVES 4

### Cucumber Raita
Peel and dice one small cucumber, place in a colander and sprinkle with salt. Leave to drain for 30 minutes, then transfer to a serving bowl. Pour 150 ml/$\frac{1}{4}$ pint yogurt over, mix lightly and sprinkle with a little chilli powder to serve.

# Summer Cutlets

*Illustrated on front cover*

*I am sure that you, too, feel that summer is not the time of year to spend hours slaving over a hot wok in the kitchen; better to cook out in the garden on a barbecue, or live on salads. But there are so many fresh foods around – all the vegetables we long for in winter, and good quality lamb – that it is a shame to miss out on them. So, if I'm going to face the kitchen, I prefer a 'let's throw it all into one pot' type dish, and here it is.*

8 lamb cutlets
1 bunch young carrots
1 kg/2 lb new potatoes
450 g/1 lb fresh unshelled peas
450 g/1 lb broccoli
225 g/8 oz pickling onions
oil for frying

salt and freshly ground black pepper
2 tablespoons chopped mint
2 tablespoons plain flour
600 ml/1 pint dry white wine
sprigs of mint to garnish

Trim any excess fat from the lamb cutlets. Trim and scrape the carrots and scrape the potatoes. Shell the peas. Trim the broccoli and break it into florets. Peel the onions.

Heat a little oil in the wok and add the cutlets, then fry them until browned all over. Remove from the wok and set aside, then add the onions. Cook these until softened, adding seasoning to taste. Stir in the mint and flour and cook for a minute, then pour in the wine and bring to the boil.

Reduce the heat and add the carrots, potatoes and peas. Return the lamb to the wok and put the lid on it, then simmer for about 20 minutes, or until the vegetables are tender. Add the broccoli for the last 5 minutes of the cooking time. Serve, garnished with the mint sprigs. SERVES 4

# Meatballs with Prawns

*Illustrated on page 90*

*Serve this oriental pork and prawn dish straight from the wok, with steamed rice or cooked egg noodles as accompaniments. Arm your guests with chopsticks and provide small bowls instead of plates.*

| | |
|---|---|
| 450 g/1 lb lean minced pork | 1 teaspoon cornflour |
| 2 tablespoons fresh breadcrumbs | 4 tablespoons dry sherry |
| 1 small egg | 4 tablespoons chicken stock |
| 2 tablespoons soy sauce | 100 g/4 oz peeled cooked prawns |
| 3 large dried Chinese mushrooms | GARNISH *(optional)* |
| 2 large spring onions | a few spring onions |
| 1 tablespoon light sesame oil | small bunch of radishes |
| 25 g/1 oz flaked almonds | $\frac{1}{4}$ cucumber |

If you are planning on garnishing the dish then prepare the ingredients for the garnish in advance. To make the ends of the spring onions curl, wash and trim off any limp parts. Leave plenty of the green part on the onions, then cut down into these to give fine strips, all attached to the white base. Place the spring onions in a bowl of ice-cold water and set aside in the refrigerator while you are cooking the dish. Spring onion curls can be prepared several hours in advance if you like; they normally take about 45 minutes to curl but this depends on the length of the onions – don't be impatient if they are not ready within an hour!

Trim the radishes. Then, using a sharp pointed knife, make a series of small V-shaped cuts round the centre of each radish, pushing the knife into the middle of each vegetable as you do so. Pull the two halves apart and set aside in a covered dish or piece of cling film. Cut the cucumber diagonally into thin slices and set these aside, again covering them to stop them drying out.

Mix the minced pork with the breadcrumbs, egg and soy sauce, then knead the mixture thoroughly so that it binds together. Shape small spoonfuls of this mixture into balls about the size of walnuts, place them on a plate and set aside.

Place the mushrooms in a small basin and cover with boiling water, then leave them to soak for 10 to 15 minutes, or until they are soft. Chop the spring onions and set aside.

Heat the oil in the wok and add the almonds. Stir-fry for a few minutes until they are lightly browned, then remove from the pan and drain on absorbent kitchen paper. Add the meatballs to the oil remaining in the pan and fry them, turning frequently, until they are browned all over. Take care when turning the meatballs that you do not break them up. While the meatballs are cooking cream the cornflour with the sherry and stock until smooth. Drain and slice the mushrooms.

When all the meatballs are cooked, add the mushrooms and chopped spring onions to the pan and cook for a few minutes. Stir in the prawns, then pour in the cornflour mixture and bring to the boil. Simmer for a few minutes. Arrange the ingredients for the garnish round the meatball mixture, either in the wok or in a heated serving dish, and serve immediately. SERVES 4

# Cumberland Pork

*Illustrated on page 92*

*Pork is an economical meat and, because it is so versatile, it does equally well for the most imaginative dishes or day-to-day ones. Here is a homely dish to serve to the family; accompany it with baked potatoes and a cauliflower gratin or simple buttered vegetables.*

1 kg/2 lb lean boneless pork (use leg, shoulder or trimmed knuckle)
450 g/1 lb pickling onions
2 tablespoons oil
4 tablespoons plain flour
salt and freshly ground black pepper

juice of 2 oranges
300 ml/$\frac{1}{2}$ pint red wine
grated rind of 1 orange
100 g/4 oz redcurrant jelly
GARNISH
orange slices
sprigs of watercress

Cut the pork into small cubes and cut any large pickling onions in half. Heat the oil in the wok and add the pork and onions, then cook, stirring frequently, until the meat is browned. Stir in the flour and seasoning and cook for a minute, then pour in the orange juice and wine. Bring to the boil, add the orange rind and redcurrant jelly and stir until the jelly dissolves. Then reduce the heat and simmer for 15 minutes, or until the meat is tender.

To serve, transfer to a heated serving dish and garnish with the orange slices and watercress sprigs. SERVES 4

# Pork Jewels

*Serve these small pork balls coated in fluffy rice on a platter, garnished with salad ingredients. Eat them as soon as they are prepared.*

175 g/6 oz round-grain (pudding) rice
450 g/1 lb lean minced pork
4 tablespoons rich soy sauce
sesame oil
1 large clove garlic

1 tablespoon grated fresh root ginger
GARNISH
sprigs of watercress
a few very small tomatoes (cherry tomatoes)
¼ cucumber

Place the rice in a sieve and rinse it thoroughly under cold running water. Transfer it to a basin and cover with cold water, then set aside to soak for 15 minutes.

Meanwhile, mix the pork with the soy sauce, a little oil, the crushed clove of garlic and the ginger. Knead all the ingredients together thoroughly so that they are well combined. Take small spoonfuls of the meat mixture and shape them into meatballs, just smaller in size than walnuts. Drain the rice and roll the meatballs in it, pressing the grains well into the meat. Place these jewels in a shallow heatproof dish, allowing enough room between them for the rice to swell as it cooks. Stand the dish on the steaming rack in the wok and pour in enough water to come up to the level of the base of the dish. Bring to the boil and put the lid on the wok, then boil steadily for 15 to 20 minutes.

While the jewels are cooking, prepare the garnish. Rinse and trim the watercress and pick out small sprigs or bunches. Cut down through the tomatoes, almost to the base, four times in all, so that the pieces open outwards. Place small sprigs of watercress in the centre of each tomato. Using a canelle knife if you have one, or the tines of a fork, score the skin of the cucumber along its length, to give a striped effect. Slice the cucumber and halve the slices.

Carefully arrange the cooked jewels on a serving platter and add the prepared garnish. Serve immediately, with any juices from the cooking dish poured over. SERVES 4

**Right** *top:* Pesto Pork (page 98); *bottom:* Veal with Salami (page 81)
**Overleaf** *clockwise, from the top:* Prawn Fried Rice (page 145), Barbecued Spare Ribs (page 93), Meatballs with Prawns (page 86), Stuffed Chinese Mushrooms (page 118)

# Barbecued Spare Ribs

*Illustrated on page 90*

*These spare ribs have an authentic Chinese flavour and if you add the red-coloured powder they will look as authentic as they taste. Serve them as a starter or as a main course, with Chinese cabbage and steamed rice.*

675 g/1½ lb pork spare ribs
600 ml/1 pint chicken stock
2 tablespoons soy sauce
3 large cloves garlic
½ teaspoon five spice powder
pinch of Chinese red powder
(optional)

2 tablespoons sesame oil
2 tablespoons concentrated tomato
purée
salt
½ medium-sized Chinese cabbage
1 bunch spring onions
2 tablespoons oil

Ask the butcher to separate the spare ribs, or separate them yourself using a meat cleaver. Place the spare ribs in the wok with the stock and stir in the soy sauce. Bring to the boil and put the lid on the wok, then reduce the heat and simmer for 30 minutes, or until the meat is tender.

While the spare ribs are cooking, prepare the sauce. Crush the garlic into a small basin and sprinkle in the five spice powder, and red powder if using. Stir in the sesame oil and tomato purée and season the mixture with a little salt.

When the spare ribs are cooked, remove them from the wok using a slotted spoon and place them on a plate. Spread the spice mixture over them so that they are all thinly covered – an old pastry brush is useful for this but remember that, if you used the red powder, the pastry brush is likely to be permanently stained. Set the ribs aside to cool while you prepare the salad ingredients. Shred the Chinese cabbage and trim the spring onions. If you like, the onions may be curled (see Meatballs with Prawns, page 86) or they can be cut into strips.

Remove the stock from the wok – this can be used for soup-making or for preparing a sauce, or it can be frozen for later use, but when it is used it will need diluting with extra water. Rinse and wipe out the wok and rub a little oil round the inside if it is carbon steel. Pour the oil into the wok and place it over a high heat. Add the spare ribs to the smoking oil and cook them quickly, turning once or twice, until crisp and well browned on all sides.

Arrange the prepared salad ingredients on a large serving platter and pile the ribs on top. Serve immediately. SERVES 4

*Top:* Cumberland Pork (page 87); *bottom:* Wok Beans (page 100)

# Pork Wun Tuns

*Wun tuns are a type of Chinese dumpling and they are made from a dough which is similar to pasta. Once prepared, you can cook wun tuns either by simmering them in liquid or by deep frying them to give crisp, light results. Filled with just a little well-flavoured meat or fish, these frilly-edged dumplings are delicious served with steamed rice.*

| | |
|---|---|
| 1 egg, beaten | FILLING |
| 1.15 litres/2 pints Rich Chicken | 100 g/4 oz lean minced pork |
| Stock (page 17) | 2 tablespoons dried shrimps |
| WUN TUN DOUGH | sesame oil |
| 50 g/2 oz plain flour | 2 teaspoons soy sauce |
| 50 g/2 oz cornflour | $\frac{1}{2}$ small onion |
| 2 teaspoons baking powder | ACCOMPANIMENT |
| pinch of salt | 1 small Chinese cabbage |
| 1 egg, lightly beaten | 1 (227-g/8-oz) can bamboo shoots |
| 2 tablespoons water | 2 carrots |
| | 4 tablespoons dry sherry |

First make the dough. Sift the flours, baking powder and salt into a mixing bowl and make a well in the centre. Add the egg and water and mix in the dry ingredients to make a stiff dough. Turn out on to a lightly floured surface and knead thoroughly until very smooth. Work quickly so that the dough does not stick to the work surface and try to avoid using lots of flour. Divide the dough in half and keep the portions covered with cling film while you prepare the filling.

Mix the pork with the shrimps, a few drops of sesame oil and the soy sauce. Chop the onion half very finely and add it to the meat mixture. Stir well to combine all the ingredients.

Back to the dough: take one portion (keep the other covered) and roll it out on a well-floured surface until it is very thin. It should form a square of about 25 cm/10 in. The thinner the dough becomes the better the results, but take great care not to rip it when you are rolling it out because it is very difficult to patch up any holes. Trim the edges and cut out nine small squares. Roll out each of these in turn to give pieces of dough which are roughly 10 cm/4 in square and very thin. Place a little filling (less than a teaspoonful) in the middle of each piece of dough and brush the edges with a little beaten egg. Gather up the dough to enclose the filling completely, sealing it in well but leaving the edges of the dough free. The filled wun tuns should look like small gathered muslin herb bags. Place the filled wun tuns on a large floured board or plate. Repeat with the second portion of dough.

Pour the stock into the wok and bring it to the boil, then reduce the heat so that it simmers very gently. Cook the wun tuns in the stock, a few at a time, for 5 minutes. Do not allow the stock to boil too rapidly or the wun tuns may break up and lose their filling. Remove the cooked wun tuns from the stock with a slotted spoon and set aside.

While the wun tuns are cooking shred the Chinese cabbage and slice the drained bamboo shoots. Cut the slices into fine strips. Cut the trimmed carrots into similar-sized strips.

When all the wun tuns are cooked bring the stock to a rapid boil in the open wok and boil hard until it has reduced by half. Add the carrot and bamboo shoot strips to the stock, with the sherry, and boil for a minute. Add the cabbage and reduce the heat, then return the wun tuns to the wok and simmer for 2 minutes to heat through. Serve straightaway. SERVES 4

# Winter Pork with Dumplings

*This is a good basic recipe to feed to the family on a cold day. In fact, the stew is quite delicious and the tasty dumplings are satisfying enough to make this dish a complete meal in itself.*

675 g/1½ lb lean boneless pork
2 onions
225 g/8 oz carrots
2 tablespoons plain flour
salt and freshly ground black pepper
25 g/1 oz dripping or lard
sprig of sage
600 ml/1 pint chicken stock

pared rind and juice of 1 orange
DUMPLINGS
175 g/6 oz self-raising flour
salt
1 tablespoon chopped fresh herbs (for example, thyme, parsley and sage)
75 g/3 oz shredded beef suet
4–5 tablespoons cold water

Cut the pork into cubes, slice the onions and carrots, and sprinkle the flour over the meat, adding plenty of seasoning. Melt the dripping or lard in the wok and add the meat, then fry, turning frequently, until well browned all over. Add the onions, carrots and sage, and continue cooking for a few minutes, until the onion is soft. Stir in any remaining flour and gradually pour in the stock. Add the orange juice, stir well and place the rind on top. Bring to the boil and reduce the heat, then put the lid on the wok and simmer for 40 minutes.

While the stew is cooking prepare the dumplings. Sift the flour into a bowl with a pinch of salt and add the herbs. Stir in the suet and add the water a few minutes before the pork has finished cooking. Shape the suet pastry into eight small round dumplings and place these lightly on top of the meat. Replace the lid of the wok and simmer for a further 10 minutes, to cook the dumplings. Serve immediately. SERVES 4

# Variations

**Pork and Olive Stew**
Omit the carrots and orange rind. Add 100 g/4 oz stuffed green olives to the meat after 30 minutes' cooking time. Make the dumplings as above, if you like, and cook them on top of the stew. Just before serving gently stir 4 tablespoons double cream into the sauce, without disturbing the dumplings.

**Mixed Pork Pot**
If you like wholesome stews full of vegetables, then this is the one for you. Add one cubed small swede and a sliced large parsnip to the stew with the carrots. Stir in 1 (397-g/14-oz) can tomatoes with the stock and add plenty of chopped fresh parsley to the sauce. Cook the dumplings as above.

# Mango Chops

*Sweet, ripe mango slices give simple pork chops an exotic image. Mixed with orange in this recipe, they make a tangy sauce to which you can add sliced banana and cooking apple if you really want to serve an unusually fruity dish. It is best to restrict the accompaniments to foods which will absorb the flavour of the sauce; try boiled rice flavoured with a couple of green cardamoms and a cinnamon stick, or boiled potatoes sprinkled with just a little chopped rosemary. Serve an ultra-simple green salad of crisp, curly endive, topped with chopped spring onions, and dressed with a little olive oil and freshly ground black pepper.*

| | |
|---|---|
| 1 large onion | 1 tablespoon oil |
| 2 ripe mangoes | 1 large clove garlic |
| 3 oranges | 2 teaspoons plain flour |
| 4 boneless pork spare rib chops | 2 tablespoons brandy (optional) |
| salt and freshly ground black pepper | chopped fresh coriander to garnish |

Thinly slice the onion and separate the slices into rings. Using a sharp pointed knife, cut round the mangoes lengthways, in as far as the large stone, then carefully cut between the stone and the flesh to remove all the fruit in two portions. Preparing a mango is fairly messy, but using this method you shouldn't lose any of the fruit. While you are cutting through the fruit hold it over a large plate to catch any juice, then pour this into the sauce with the other ingredients. Cut the peel from the mangoes and slice the flesh fairly thickly. Grate the rind from one of the oranges and squeeze the juice from all three. Trim any excess fat from the chops and season them to taste.

Heat the oil in the wok and crush the garlic into it. Add the chops and cook them over high heat, turning them round once and over once or twice, until they are well browned and cooked through. Remove the chops from the wok and arrange them on a warmed serving platter; keep hot. Add the onion to the fat remaining in the pan and cook until soft but not browned. Stir in the flour, cook for a minute, then add the orange rind and mango slices, with just a little more seasoning. Pour in the orange juice (and any mango juice) and bring to the boil, then pour in the brandy, if using, and cook for a few seconds. Pour this sauce over the chops, using a spoon to arrange the slices of mango. Sprinkle with a little chopped fresh coriander and serve immediately. SERVES 4

# Pesto Pork

*Illustrated on page 89*

*Pesto is a full-flavoured sauce served with pasta in the Genoa region of Italy. It is made from fresh basil, pine nuts, garlic and fresh Parmesan cheese, with olive oil to moisten the mixture. Here, it turns a simple dish of pork and potatoes into something very special.*

4 thin pork steaks, cut from the leg
4 large potatoes
450 g/1 lb French beans
oil for frying
salt and freshly ground black pepper

PESTO SAUCE
a large handful of fresh basil
2 large cloves garlic
2 tablespoons pine nuts
2 tablespoons freshly grated Parmesan cheese
150 ml/$\frac{1}{4}$ pint olive oil

Trim the fat off the pork and set the steaks aside. Cut the potatoes in half and place them on the steaming rack in the wok. Pour in enough water to come up to the level of the rack without touching the potatoes, then bring to the boil and cover the wok. Reduce the heat slightly so that the water simmers quite hard and steam the potatoes for 25 to 30 minutes, or until they are tender. Meanwhile trim the French beans and add them to the steaming rack for the last 10 minutes of the steaming time. Set the cooked vegetables aside, pour the water out of the wok and wipe it dry, greasing it if necessary.

While the vegetables are cooking prepare the pesto sauce. Trim any large stalks off the basil (small ones don't matter) and place the leaves in a liquidiser. Add the crushed garlic and nuts (you can omit these as they are rather expensive, and you will still have a well-flavoured sauce without them) and sprinkle in the cheese. Pour a little of the olive oil into the liquidiser and process until a smooth paste is formed, then gradually pour in the remaining oil as the ingredients are processed.

Heat just a little oil in the wok and add the pork, then fry the slices until browned on both sides. Meanwhile, slice the potatoes thickly. When the pork is almost cooked, remove the slices from the wok and lay the potato slices in the pan, seasoning them very lightly. Arrange the French beans on top and lay the pork, overlapping, on top of them. Put the lid on the wok and cook gently until the vegetables are heated through – this should take about 10 minutes.

To serve, pour a little of the pesto sauce down the middle of the pork and offer the rest separately. SERVES 4

# Bacon Roly-poly

*It is easier to make a suet pastry roll than it is to line, fill and wrap a pudding basin, and the steaming rack of the wok is wide enough to accommodate a roly-poly. This bacon roll is deliciously warming and satisfying on cold winter days – I tested it on a very hot July morning and even then I ate more of it than I would wish to admit! If you like, you can cook some vegetables – carrots, parsnips or Brussels sprouts – in the steaming water. Add them towards the end of the cooking time and remember to add salt.*

350 g/12 oz smoked streaky bacon
1 large onion
100 g/4 oz button mushrooms
salt and freshly ground black pepper
$\frac{1}{2}$ teaspoon rubbed sage

$\frac{1}{2}$ teaspoon dried thyme
SUET PASTRY
225 g/8 oz self-raising flour
100 g/4 oz shredded beef suet
pinch of salt
scant 150 ml/$\frac{1}{4}$ pint water

First prepare the filling. Cut the rinds off the bacon and finely chop the rashers. Finely chop the onion and slice the mushrooms. Mix all these prepared ingredients together and add a little seasoning – not too much salt because the bacon may already be quite salty. Stir in the herbs and set aside. Butter a large piece of foil to hold the roll.

To make the pastry, sift the flour into a bowl and add the suet. Stir in well and add a pinch of salt. Use a round-bladed knife or a fork to mix the ingredients and gradually pour in the water to make a soft dough. Turn out on to a floured surface and knead together very lightly and quickly, then roll out to give an oblong measuring about 25 × 20 cm/10 × 8 in. Try to keep the pastry to a fairly even thickness so that you do not end up with any particularly stodgy areas when you cut the slices.

Arrange the filling in an even layer on the pastry, taking it to within about 1 cm/$\frac{1}{2}$ in of the edge. Dampen the edges of the pastry very lightly then roll up to enclose the filling and press the edges together to seal. Carefully lift the roll on to the prepared foil and wrap it loosely, to allow for rising, but securely, to prevent any steam from entering. Stand the roll on the steaming rack in the wok and pour in enough water to come up as far as the rack. Bring to the boil and put the lid on the wok, then boil steadily for 1$\frac{1}{2}$ hours. Check to make sure that the water does not boil dry during cooking and add any vegetables 10 to 20 minutes before the roll is cooked.

To serve, carefully lift the roll off the rack and open the foil. Fold it back and slide the roll on to a warmed serving plate. Arrange cooked vegetables round the sides and serve immediately. SERVES 4

# Wok Beans

*Illustrated on page 92*

*Here is a particularly quick bean-pot recipe made with a couple of cans of beans and some cooked ham. You can, if you like, use frankfurters, smoked Dutch sausage or cold roast pork instead of the ham – in fact, it's just the recipe for using up any tasty leftovers of meat or vegetables.*

2 onions
450 g/1 lb cooked ham, in one piece
50 g/2 oz butter
2 cloves garlic
225 g/8 oz sweet corn
2 (425-g/15-oz) cans red kidney beans

1 (397-g/14-oz) can tomatoes
3 tablespoons concentrated tomato purée
bay leaf
1 teaspoon dried mixed herbs
salt and freshly ground black pepper

Finely chop the onions and cut the ham into cubes. Melt the butter in the wok and crush the garlic into it. Add the onion and fry until it is soft but not browned. Stir in the ham, sweet corn and both cans of beans, with the juice from just one can. Add the tomatoes, tomato purée, bay leaf and herbs and stir well to dissolve the purée. Bring to the boil and add salt and pepper to taste. Reduce the heat and simmer the bean-pot for 3 minutes.

Serve in individual bowls or straight from the wok, and offer a salad of mixed green vegetables and some crusty bread as accompaniments. SERVES 4

*Top:* Courgettes with Feta (page 107); *bottom:* Cabbage Braise (page 106)

# Crisp Liver with Orange Sauce

*Liver is not one of my favourite foods, but I did enjoy the contrast between
the liver and the crisp coating in this dish; the tangy orange sauce provided
just the right complement for the rich liver. Serve the slices with a fairly
plain salad and new potatoes or creamed old potatoes.*

1 large onion
1 teaspoon rubbed sage
1 teaspoon dried thyme
50 g/2 oz dried breadcrumbs
8 slices lamb's liver
4 tablespoons plain flour
salt and freshly ground black
pepper

1 large egg, beaten
25 g/1 oz butter *or* 1 tablespoon
oil
grated rind and juice of 1 orange
300 ml/½ pint chicken stock
GARNISH
1 orange, sliced
watercress sprigs

Thinly slice the onion. Mix the sage with the thyme and breadcrumbs, and
sprinkle this mixture on to a large plate. Coat the liver in the flour and
sprinkle over plenty of seasoning, then dip the slices in the beaten egg and
coat them in the breadcrumb mixture, pressing it on well.

Heat the butter or oil in the wok and fry the liver in it, turning once, until
browned and crisp on both sides. Drain on absorbent kitchen paper and
arrange on a serving dish. Keep hot while you prepare the sauce.

Add the onion slices to the fat remaining in the wok and cook until soft but
not browned. Stir in the orange rind and juice and pour in the stock. Bring to
the boil and boil for 2 to 3 minutes, or until slightly thickened.

Garnish the liver with orange slices and watercress sprigs and serve the
sauce separately. SERVES 4

*Top:* New Potato Curry (page 110); *bottom:* Gobhi Masala (page 114)

# Vegetable Dishes

*Fresh vegetables are brought to their full flavour value when cooked quickly for slightly crisp results, and stir-frying is by far the best way to give them that particular zest. But there is far more to cooking vegetables in a wok than shredding and tossing; layered in supper dishes, stuffed for main meals, seasoned, spiced and moistened with flavoursome sauces, even the most modest of vegetables becomes worthy of a gourmet's table.*

*So glimpse through these recipes next time you want to surprise the family or friends with a tasty supper-time treat. Served straight from the wok, lots of these dishes save on washing up too! Why not blow convention to the winds and serve a new potato curry as the centre-piece of a meal? The recipe is here, with a list of suitable side dishes to complete the menu. For vegetarians there are several dishes to serve for the main course – Courgettes with Feta, Aubergines with Paneer, and Pipérade, for example. And if you're looking for an interesting starter, try the mushrooms fried in breadcrumbs and served with a garlic-laced banana sauce.*

*Now that you have this chapter to turn to you need never be at a loss for ideas next time your total food store amounts to just a bag of potatoes and a few tins in the cupboard. Have fun with these recipes and try your favourite vegetables in dishes that you will delight in serving to your guests as well as to the family.*

# Ratatouille

*As well as making an excellent accompaniment for grilled or barbecued meats and fish, ratatouille can be served as a first course with crisp French bread and butter.*

| | |
|---|---|
| 2 large aubergines | 675 g/1½ lb tomatoes |
| salt and freshly ground black pepper | 6 tablespoons olive oil |
| | 2 cloves garlic |
| 4 courgettes | 4 tablespoons chopped parsley |
| 2 onions | 150 ml/¼ pint robust red wine |

Trim off and discard the ends of the aubergines and cut them into chunks. Place the chunks in a colander and sprinkle with salt, then set aside for 20 minutes, standing them over a plate or bowl.

Meanwhile, trim off and discard the ends of the courgettes and cut them into thick slices. Slice the onions fairly thickly and separate the slices into rings. Place the tomatoes in a bowl and cover with boiling water, leave for 30 seconds to a minute, then drain and peel. Cut the peeled tomatoes into quarters. When the aubergines have stood for the required length of time, shake off any excess moisture and dry them thoroughly on absorbent kitchen paper.

Heat the oil in the wok and add the onion rings. Cook for a minute, then stir in the aubergines and crush the garlic over them. Cook for a few minutes, stirring frequently, until the oil has been absorbed and the aubergines are beginning to soften. Add the courgettes and tomatoes and sprinkle plenty of freshly ground black pepper over the vegetables. Add just a little salt but remember that the aubergines will already be quite salty. Sprinkle the parsley over, then pour in the wine. Heat gently to boiling point, give the vegetables a stir and put the lid on the wok. Reduce the heat so that the casserole simmers gently and cook for 20 to 30 minutes, or until all the vegetables are tender. Serve in a heated dish or straight from the wok.
SERVES 4

# Cabbage Braise

*Illustrated on page 101*

*Plain boiled cabbage can be very boring, but this cabbage dish is quite exciting – it's saucy and well flavoured with other vegetables, and is in no way reminiscent of the soggy cabbage most people suffered for their school dinners. Serve the crisp wedges of cabbage with the crunchy topping and plenty of warm bread for supper, or omit the topping and serve them to accompany those meat or fish dishes which do not have a sauce.*

1 (1-kg/2-lb) savoy cabbage
1 onion
2 carrots
2 sticks celery
50 g/2 oz butter
salt and freshly ground black pepper
1 tablespoon plain flour

300 ml/$\frac{1}{2}$ pint chicken stock
TOPPING *(optional)*
350 g/12 oz lean bacon rashers
3 slices bread
50 g/2 oz butter
2 tablespoons chopped parsley
100 g/4 oz Lancashire or Caerphilly cheese

Trim the tough outside leaves and stalks off the cabbage and cut the cabbage into four wedges. Wash and drain these thoroughly. Chop the onion and dice the carrots and celery.

If you are going to serve the topping, then prepare it before cooking the cabbage. Cut the rinds off the bacon and chop the rashers. Cut the crusts off the bread and cut the slices into small cubes. Melt the butter in the wok and fry the cubes of bread in it until golden brown, then remove from the pan and drain on absorbent kitchen paper. Add the bacon to the wok and fry until cooked but not crisp. Remove the bacon with a slotted spoon and mix it with the croûtons (fried cubes of bread) and parsley. When cool, stir in the cheese.

To cook the cabbage, melt the butter in the wok and add the onion, carrots, celery and seasoning. Fry until the onion is soft but not browned. Stir in the flour and cook for a minute, then pour in the stock and bring to the boil. Place the wedges of cabbage in the sauce and spoon a little of it over them. Put the lid on the wok and simmer steadily for 25 to 30 minutes, or until the cabbage is cooked to your liking.

Sprinkle the topping (if used) over the cabbage and serve immediately.
SERVES 4

# Courgettes with Feta

*Illustrated on page 101*

*Serve these courgettes as a first course, or as a light lunch or supper dish
with warmed pita bread. Alternatively, serve them as an accompaniment to
grilled or barbecued lamb chops, or simply fry the chops in your wok first
and keep them hot while you quickly prepare the courgettes.*

4 large courgettes
175 g/6 oz feta cheese, chilled
4 tablespoons olive oil
1 or 2 cloves garlic

salt and freshly ground black
pepper
3 tablespoons chopped fresh basil
1 lemon, cut into wedges, to
garnish

Trim the ends off the courgettes and peel the courgettes very lightly – they
should be a dark green when a very thin layer of peel is cut off. Cut each
courgette lengthways into quarters. Crumble the feta cheese, then return it
to the refrigerator because it has to be very cold to complement the fried
courgettes.

Heat the oil in the wok and crush the garlic into it; if you are keen on foods
which are well flavoured with garlic, then use two cloves. Add the
courgettes, season lightly, and fry them quickly until lightly browned. The
heat should be high enough to brown the courgettes before they lose their
crisp texture. Transfer the courgettes to a heated serving platter and sprinkle
the chilled feta cheese over. Top with the basil and pour on the oil from the
wok. Arrange the lemon wedges round the courgettes and serve immediately. The combination of flavours and textures in this dish is delicious!
SERVES 4

# Porcisson Courgettes

*This dish is quite substantial enough to serve on its own, with some fresh bread, for lunch or supper. The courgettes cook particularly quickly and the French pork sausage, flavoured with red wine, herbs and spices, adds both flavour and texture. You can also use good-quality salami if you like.*

1 (225-g/8-oz) dried saucisson (cooked French sausage, flavoured with garlic, herbs and red wine)
450 g/1 lb courgettes
olive oil

4 tablespoons chopped parsley
2 tablespoons chopped chives
salt and freshly ground black pepper

Slice the saucisson and trim and slice the courgettes. Grease the wok with just a little oil and heat it over a high heat. Add the saucisson and courgette slices and cook, tossing frequently, until the courgettes are lightly cooked, that is tender but still crisp.

Sprinkle the herbs over, taste and adjust the seasoning if necessary, then serve immediately. SERVES 4

# Creamed Mushrooms and Potatoes

*Although this potato casserole tastes best made with new potatoes, it can also be made with old potatoes; quarter any that are very large.*

1 kg/2 lb small new potatoes
50 g/2 oz butter
salt and freshly ground black pepper
1 tablespoon plain flour
300 ml/$\frac{1}{2}$ pint chicken stock

225 g/8 oz small button mushrooms
300 ml/$\frac{1}{2}$ pint single cream
2 tablespoons chopped parsley to garnish

Scrape the potatoes. Melt the butter in the wok, add the potatoes and seasoning to taste, and cook for a few minutes, turning frequently. Then stir in the flour and gradually pour in the stock. Bring to the boil, reduce the heat and put the lid on the wok. Simmer gently, turning the potatoes occasionally to make sure they cook evenly, for about 20 to 30 minutes, or until the potatoes are tender. (They take longer than normal to cook because they are not covered in boiling water.)

When the potatoes are tender, stir the mushrooms into the sauce and cook for a minute. Then stir in the cream and heat through gently without boiling. Sprinkle the parsley over before serving. SERVES 4

# Summertime Potatoes

*Illustrated on page 119*

*New potatoes are so delicious that I feel quite justified in making them the focus point of the meal. This is a dish for when you're feeling extravagant because prawns are rather expensive, but if you want to make a more economical hot salad, try some of the variations below. Serve with brown bread and butter and a green salad.*

| | |
|---|---|
| 1 kg/2 lb small new potatoes | 2 teaspoons chopped mint |
| 600 ml/1 pint chicken stock | 2 tablespoons chopped parsley |
| 350 g/12 oz cooked ham | 1 tablespoon white wine vinegar |
| 450 g/1 lb peeled cooked prawns | salt and freshly ground black |
| 4 spring onions | pepper |

Scrub or scrape the potatoes and place in the wok. Add the stock and bring to the boil, then cover the wok and reduce the heat so the liquid simmers steadily. Cook for 15 minutes, or until tender.

While the potatoes are cooking cut the ham into small dice and mix with the prawns. Chop the spring onions and mix these with the herbs. Using a slotted spoon, remove the cooked potatoes from the wok. Bring the stock to the boil in the open wok and boil rapidly until it is reduced by half. Add the vinegar to the stock and stir in the ham and prawns. Return the potatoes to the wok and heat through gently for a minute, then add the herbs and spring onions. Stir well to combine all the ingredients and taste and adjust the seasoning, adding some freshly ground black pepper and a little salt to taste. Serve immediately. SERVES 4

# Variations

**Tunatime Potatoes**
(A funny title but a delicious combination of ingredients!) Omit the prawns and ham and add 2 (198-g/7-oz) cans tuna fish, drained and flaked. Stir in 1 tablespoon chopped capers, if you like, and add 4 quartered hard-boiled eggs. Use 2 tablespoons chopped tarragon instead of the mint. This is an excellent standby if you keep cans of fish in stock, and it can also be prepared with cubed old potatoes.

**New Potatoes with Bacon**
Omit the prawns and ham from the basic recipe. Roughly chop 450 g/1 lb rindless, smoked streaky bacon and dry-fry it in the wok until crisp before you cook the potatoes. Drain the bacon on absorbent kitchen paper and set aside. Add the bacon to the stock instead of the prawns and ham, and use 2 teaspoons chopped fresh thyme instead of the mint. Serve with a bowl of grated Gruyère cheese.

# New Potato Curry

*Illustrated on page 102*

*This curry is superb! The potatoes absorb the flavour of the spices and, if they are not overcooked, their texture and taste is perfectly complemented by the tangy yogurt sauce. For a complete change serve this curry as the main dish and prepare a selection of side dishes to go with it. Serve the potato curry straight from the wok, keeping it hot over a fondue burner turned down very low, or on a plate warmer.*

2 large onions
1 kg/2 lb small new potatoes
50 g/2 oz fresh root ginger
2 cloves garlic
50 g/2 oz ghee (page 113) or butter
2 bay leaves
1 stick cinnamon
2 teaspoons fennel seeds
3 green cardamoms

1 teaspoon turmeric
600 ml/1 pint water
salt and freshly ground black pepper
300 ml/$\frac{1}{2}$ pint natural yogurt
GARNISH
chilli powder to taste
chopped fresh coriander leaves

Finely chop the onions and scrape the potatoes (you can use old potatoes if you like but the flavour is not quite as good). Grate the ginger and crush the garlic and mix both together. Melt the ghee in the wok and add the onion, ginger mixture, bay leaves, broken cinnamon stick, fennel seeds, cardamoms and turmeric. Fry, stirring continuously, until the onion is soft but not browned. Stir in the potatoes, pour in the water and add salt and pepper to taste, then bring to the boil and cover the wok. Simmer steadily for 10 minutes, then uncover the wok and cook fairly rapidly for a further 10 minutes, or until most of the water has evaporated.

Pour the yogurt over the potatoes and heat through fairly gently, to avoid curdling the sauce. Sprinkle chilli powder to taste and coriander over before serving the curry with any of the accompaniments suggested below.
SERVES 4

# Accompaniments

Peeled cooked prawns, sprinkled with a little grated lemon rind and chilli powder.
Bombay ducks (strongly flavoured dried fish), grilled until crisp and served with lemon wedges.
Chopped cooked chicken, sprinkled with toasted flaked almonds and chopped chillies.
Crisp bacon rolls – although these are not a typical accompaniment for Indian food they taste delicious with potato curry!

Quartered hard-boiled eggs, sprinkled with a mixture of paprika, a little chopped fresh thyme and salt and pepper.

Peeled green and red peppers, chopped and sprinkled with a little crushed garlic and oil. (To peel peppers, hold them on a fork over a gas flame, or cook them under a very hot grill until the skin is blistered, then rub off the skin under cold running water.)

Wedges of cucumber, sprinkled with a pinch each of ground cloves and chilli powder.

Quartered tomatoes, sprinkled with thinly sliced onion rings.

A selection of Indian breads and chutneys – for example, chapatis, papadums or naans, and lime pickle, mango chutney, peach chutney and either of the fresh chutneys given in the chapter on Side Dishes and Snacks.

# Potato and Salami Layer

*Illustrated on page 119*

*This makes a satisfying and tasty supper dish. You can use any cold sliced meats or sausages instead of the German salami – try other types of mild salami, ham sausage, tongue or hot and spicy Spanish salami, for example.*

675 g/1½ lb potatoes
2 large onions
50 g/2 oz butter
salt and freshly ground black pepper

2 tablespoons chopped mixed fresh herbs
2 gherkins
2 canned pimientos
225 g/8 oz German salami, thinly sliced

Thinly slice the potatoes and onions, separating the onions into rings. Melt the butter in the wok and fry the onions for a minute. Remove them from the wok and add a layer of potatoes to the pan. Top with some of the onions, plenty of seasoning and a sprinkling of fresh herbs. Continue layering the potatoes and onions with the herbs until they are all used. Put the lid on the wok and cook over medium heat for about 45 minutes, or until the potatoes are cooked. Make sure that the heat is not too fierce or the potatoes at the bottom will overcook.

Meanwhile, slice the gherkins lengthways and cut the pimientos into fine strips. Arrange the salami, gherkins and pimiento strips on top of the potatoes, re-cover the wok and cook for a few minutes more. Serve straight from the wok. SERVES 4

# Okra with Tomatoes

*Illustrated on page 50*

*Serve this lightly spiced vegetable mixture as an accompaniment to curries, or with simple grilled, fried or barbecued meats.*

| | |
|---|---|
| 450 g/1 lb okra | 4 green cardamoms |
| 450 g/1 lb tomatoes | salt and freshly ground black |
| 1 small onion | pepper |
| 75 g/3 oz ghee (page 113) *or* | 1 teaspoon garam masala |
| 25 g/1 oz butter and 2 tablespoons | 2 tablespoons chopped fresh |
| oil | coriander leaves |

Trim off and discard the ends of the okra and slice them into chunks. Place the tomatoes in a large bowl and pour in enough boiling water to cover them. Allow to stand for 30 seconds to a minute, then drain and peel them. Thinly slice the onion and quarter the peeled tomatoes.

Melt the ghee or butter and oil in the wok and add the cardamoms. Fry these for a few seconds, then add the onion and a little salt and pepper and cook until soft but not browned. Add the okra and tomatoes and cook for a few minutes, stirring the vegetables frequently. The okra should be tender but take care not to overcook them because then they become slimy and unpleasant in texture.

As soon as the vegetables are cooked, sprinkle on the garam masala and chopped coriander and serve immediately. SERVES 4

# Aubergines with Paneer

*These spiced aubergines with Indian cheese are delicious and they can be served either as an accompaniment to meat curries or on their own with boiled rice, Indian breads and chutneys, or a raita such as Cucumber Raita page 85.*

| | |
|---|---|
| 450 g/1 lb Paneer (page 156) | 75 g/3 oz ghee (see below) |
| 4 large aubergines | 3 cloves garlic |
| salt | 1 tablespoon garam masala |
| 4 green chillies | 4 tablespoons chopped fresh |
| 2 onions | coriander leaves |

Make and press the paneer according to the recipe instructions, then cut it into neat cubes and chill thoroughly. Trim off and discard the ends of the aubergines and cut them into chunks. Place the pieces of aubergine in a colander or sieve and sprinkle with salt, then leave to stand over a plate or bowl for 20 to 30 minutes. Meanwhile, cut the stalks off the chillies, remove all their seeds and pith and chop the green part finely. Finely chop the onions.

Heat the ghee in the wok and crush the garlic into it. Add the chillies and onions and cook until the onion is soft but not browned. Dry the aubergines with absorbent kitchen paper and add them to the wok with the garam masala. Cook, stirring frequently, until the aubergines are tender. Stir in the cubes of paneer and cook, without stirring at all, for a minute or two. Sprinkle the coriander over the aubergines and serve immediately. SERVES 4

**Ghee**
To prepare ghee, melt 225 g/8 oz butter (preferably unsalted) in a saucepan over a low heat. Simmer the melted fat gently for 20 to 30 minutes, by which time a sediment should have formed in the base of the pan and the excess moisture will have evaporated from the butter. Strain this clarified butter through a piece of muslin, a coffee filter paper or a double thickness of absorbent kitchen paper placed in a sieve. Cool and store in the refrigerator – the ghee will keep for several weeks.

# Gobhi Masala

*Illustrated on page 102*

*Cauliflower in a rich and spicy sauce is quite delicious. Serve Paneer Pullao (page 139) as an accompaniment, with bowls of chopped roasted cashew nuts, quartered hard-boiled eggs, Indian breads and chutneys. Alternatively, the cauliflower can be served to complement a fairly dry meat or poultry curry.*

| | |
|---|---|
| 1 large cauliflower | 1 tablespoon mustard seeds |
| 2 onions | 2 tablespoons poppy seeds |
| 50 g/2 oz fresh root ginger | $\frac{1}{2}$ teaspoon turmeric |
| 2 cloves garlic | 450 g/1 lb tomatoes |
| 4 green chillies | 3 tablespoons concentrated tomato |
| bay leaf | purée |
| 4 green cardamoms | 150 ml/$\frac{1}{4}$ pint water |
| 1 clove | 50 g/2 oz ghee (page 113) or butter |
| 1 stick cinnamon | 300 ml/$\frac{1}{2}$ pint natural yogurt |

Trim the outer green leaves and stalks from the cauliflower and wash it thoroughly under cold running water. Then place it on the steaming rack in the wok and add water to come up to the level of the rack but without touching the cauliflower. Bring to the boil and put the lid on the wok, then reduce the heat and simmer steadily for 15 minutes. The cauliflower should still be crisp when steamed.

Meanwhile, chop the onions, grate the ginger and crush the garlic. Cut the stalk ends off the chillies and remove the seeds and pith, then chop the green part finely. In a small, heavy-based frying pan, roast the bay leaf with the cardamoms, clove, broken cinnamon stick and mustard and poppy seeds over a low heat until they give off a strong aroma. Do not overcook the spices or they will taste very bitter. When the spices are ready, remove them from the pan and cool slightly, then grind them to a powder in a liquidiser. Add half the chopped onion and the ginger and garlic, then process to form a paste. Mix in the turmeric.

Place the tomatoes in a large bowl and cover them with boiling water. Leave to stand for 30 seconds to a minute, then drain and peel them. Cut the peeled tomatoes into quarters. Stir the tomato purée into the water and set aside.

When the cauliflower is ready, remove it from the wok and pour away the water. Wipe out the wok and grease it if necessary, then add the ghee and melt it over a medium heat. Add the remaining chopped onion and the chillies and cook, stirring frequently, until soft but not browned. Stir in the paste and cook, stirring frequently, for about 5 minutes. Meanwhile break the cauliflower into florets.

Pour the dissolved tomato purée into the wok and add the tomato quarters. Bring to the boil and simmer for 5 minutes, then stir in the yogurt and add the cauliflower florets. Stir well to coat the florets in the sauce but try to avoid breaking them up. Cover the wok and simmer gently for 15 minutes. When ready the cauliflower should be soft but not mushy. Serve immediately. SERVES 4

# Crunchy-topped Cauliflower

*Cauliflower can be steamed with ease and success in the wok, and it has a far better texture than boiled cauliflower. Here it is complemented by a tasty, crisp topping to make a simple supper dish.*

| | |
|---|---|
| 1 medium-sized cauliflower | salt and freshly ground black |
| 1 large onion | pepper |
| 225 g/8 oz lean bacon rashers | 2 tablespoons grated Parmesan |
| 50 g/2 oz walnuts | cheese |
| 75 g/3 oz butter | 2 tablespoons chopped parsley |

Trim the outer green leaves and stalks from the cauliflower and wash it thoroughly under cold running water. Cut a small cross into the thick base and stand the cauliflower on the steaming rack in the wok. Pour in enough water to come up to the rack without touching the cauliflower. Bring to the boil, reduce the heat slightly so that the water does not boil too rapidly, and put the lid on the wok. Cook for 20 minutes, or until the cauliflower is tender.

Meanwhile, chop the onion. Cut the rinds off the bacon and chop the rashers. Chop the walnuts. When the cauliflower is cooked, transfer it to a heated serving dish and keep hot. Pour the water from the wok and wipe it dry. Add the butter and melt it over a medium heat, then fry the onion, bacon and walnuts together until the bacon is brown. Add seasoning to taste and stir in the Parmesan cheese and parsley. Spoon this mixture over the cauliflower, with all the buttery juices, and serve immediately. SERVES 4

# Simple Chop Suey

*This quick stir-fry vegetable dish is an excellent side dish for serving with deep-fried Chinese dishes like Sweet and Sour Pork (page 65) or Barbecued Spare Ribs (page 93). Alternatively, try the Pork Chop Suey variation which follows this recipe and serve it as a main dish, with rice.*

| | |
|---|---|
| 1 small onion | 1 tablespoon sunflower oil |
| 2 carrots | 1 small clove garlic |
| 1 (227-g/8-oz) can bamboo shoots | 3–4 tablespoons soy sauce |
| 350 g/12 oz bean sprouts | |

Halve the onion, then cut it into very thin slices and separate the slices into strips. Trim the carrots and cut them into very fine strips, and do the same with the drained bamboo shoots. Pick over the bean sprouts, removing any which are slightly brown and as many of the green pods as possible.

Heat the oil in the wok and crush the garlic into it, then add the onion and carrots. Stir-fry for a few minutes, or until the onion has softened slightly. Stir in the bamboo shoots and cook for a minute, then add the bean sprouts and stir-fry for another minute before adding soy sauce to taste. Serve immediately – the bean sprouts should be very crunchy and overcooking will destroy their texture. SERVES 4

# Variation

**Pork Chop Suey**
Finely shred 350 g/12 oz lean boneless pork and fry it in the oil with the garlic until browned. Continue as above.

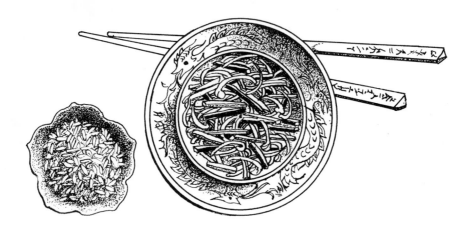

# Crispy Mushrooms with Banana Sauce

*If the thought of mushrooms with a banana sauce sounds a little bizarre to you, don't worry! I tasted this sauce when a friend prepared dinner for us one evening – she kept us guessing for some time as to what was in the deliciously creamy, spicy dressing that she had conjured up. Served with freshly cooked bacon or ham these mushrooms are superb, and they turn cold baked or boiled ham, or roasted pork, into an exciting meal. They also make an interesting starter, or a vegetarian meal when served with brown rice with walnuts.*

450 g/1 lb button mushrooms
1 large egg, beaten
about 175 g/6 oz dry white breadcrumbs
900 ml/1½ pints oil for deep frying
SAUCE
2 large ripe bananas
1 or 2 large cloves garlic
150 ml/¼ pint mayonnaise

150 ml/¼ pint single cream
salt and freshly ground black pepper
freshly grated nutmeg
paprika
GARNISH
1 crisp lettuce heart
lemon wedges
watercress sprigs (optional)

Trim the mushrooms so that they do not have any particularly long stalks, then dip them in the beaten egg and coat them in the breadcrumbs. Chill the coated mushrooms while preparing the sauce.

Mash the bananas and crushed garlic with the mayonnaise, then stir in the cream. Add salt and pepper to taste and a little grated nutmeg, then pour the sauce into a serving dish and sprinkle a little paprika over the top. Chill until required.

Pour the oil for deep frying into the wok and heat it to 190 C/375 F. Fry the mushrooms, a few at a time, until the coating is crisp and golden, then drain them on absorbent kitchen paper and keep hot until they are all cooked.

To serve, arrange the lettuce leaves on a shallow dish or plate and pile the mushrooms on top. Garnish with lemon wedges, and a few sprigs of watercress if you like, then serve immediately, with the sauce handed separately. SERVES 4

**Note**  For an informal starter or party dish, place the bowl of sauce on a large platter and arrange the crisp mushrooms, on the lettuce, round the sauce. Have tiny dishes of cocktail sticks to hand and encourage your guests to dip the mushrooms in the sauce.

# Stuffed Chinese Mushrooms

*Illustrated on page 90*

*Choose quite large dried mushrooms for this dish and serve them simply, on shredded Chinese cabbage and spring onions as a starter, or as part of a complete Chinese menu. They can be steamed over rice dishes, for example over Prawn Fried Rice (page 145), or over braised dishes. Alternatively, they can be steamed before any other dishes are prepared and then quickly reheated over steam for a few minutes before serving.*

16 large dried Chinese mushrooms
450 g/1 lb lean minced pork
2 tablespoons rich soy sauce
sesame oil
generous pinch of ground ginger

16 peeled cooked prawns
GARNISH *(optional)*
1 small bunch spring onions
a few radishes
1 bunch watercress

Place the mushrooms in a basin and cover them with boiling water, then leave to stand for 30 minutes. Meanwhile, mix the pork with the soy sauce, a few drops of sesame oil and the ginger, making sure that the ingredients are thoroughly combined.

If you wish to garnish the dish, then this would be a good time to trim the spring onions and make them into curls (see Meatballs with Prawns, page 86). Trim the radishes and cut down through them several times, to give small wedges all attached at the base. Place these radish flowers in a bowl of iced water and set in the refrigerator. Trim the watercress and choose eight neat sprigs to set aside.

Drain the soaked mushrooms and divide the filling equally between eight of them, then press the remaining eight mushrooms on top. Press the mushrooms well together between the palms of your hands – hold them over a plate as you do this because a little water may be squeezed out. Place the stuffed mushrooms on a deep plate (one with a rim) or in a shallow dish and stand it on the steaming rack in the wok. Pour in enough water to come up to the level of the rack and bring to the boil, then reduce the heat and simmer rapidly, with the lid on the wok, for 20 minutes. Place two peeled prawns on top of each mushroom, re-cover the wok and simmer for a further 5 minutes.

To serve, transfer the mushrooms to a heated serving dish and pour a little of the liquid from the plate over them. Garnish each mushroom with a tiny sprig of watercress placed between the prawns, and arrange the spring onion curls and radish flowers between and around the mushrooms on the plate. Serve immediately. SERVES 4

*Top:* Summertime Potatoes (page 109); *bottom:* Potato and Salami Layer
(page 111)

# Stuffed Cabbage with Rice

*This stuffed cabbage is moist and meaty, and the rice with vegetables which is cooked round it make this dish a complete meal.*

1 (1-kg/2-lb) savoy cabbage
100 g/4 oz streaky bacon rashers
1 onion
25 g/1 oz butter
225 g/8 oz lean minced beef
salt and freshly ground black pepper
2 tablespoons chopped parsley
2 teaspoons chopped fresh thyme
dash of Worcestershire sauce
600 ml/1 pint beef stock
225 g/8 oz long-grain rice
1 (200-g/7-oz) can pimientos
100 g/4 oz sweet corn

Cut the very top off the cabbage and trim the stalk end, removing any large outer leaves. Using a sharp pointed knife, cut the middle out of the cabbage, leaving a shell about three leaves thick. Cut the rinds off the bacon and chop the rashers. Chop the onion.

Melt the butter in the wok and add the bacon and onion. Cook until the onion is soft but not browned then add the beef and continue frying, breaking the meat up as it cooks, until lightly browned. Add seasoning to taste and the herbs, together with the Worcestershire sauce.

Use the meat mixture to stuff the cabbage, pressing it well down into the cavity. If the outside leaves of the cabbage feel rather loose, then tie a piece of string round it to make sure it stays together during cooking. Place the cabbage in the wok and pour in the stock. Bring to the boil, put the lid on the wok and reduce the heat so that the stock simmers gently. Cook for 45 minutes, or until the cabbage is tender.

After 25 minutes' cooking time add the rice to the stock surrounding the cabbage, stirring it in lightly. While the rice is cooking, chop the drained pimientos and mix with the sweet corn. Add these vegetables to the rice 5 minutes before the end of the cooking time. Make sure that the stock does not dry up during cooking, adding more if necessary.

Serve the cabbage and rice straight from the wok if you like, having first removed any string from the cabbage. Cut the cabbage into four wedges to serve. SERVES 4

*Top:* Pipérade (page 125); *bottom:* Dolmades (page 122)

# Dolmades

*Illustrated on page 120*

*These stuffed vine leaves are delicious served either hot or cold, with a salad of crisp lettuce, cucumber, black olives and feta cheese. In addition offer a basket of warmed pita bread to mop up the thin sauce in which the dolmades are cooked. The wok is ideal for preparing these little packages because they can be arranged round the sides of the pan and you can cook enough for up to ten servings all at once.*

about 30 canned or packeted vine leaves
1 large onion
1 tablespoon olive oil
2 cloves garlic
salt and freshly ground black pepper
450 g/1 lb lean minced lamb
2 teaspoons dried marjoram

SAUCE
300 ml/½ pint chicken stock
1 (397-g/14-oz) can tomatoes
2 tablespoons concentrated tomato purée
300 ml/½ pint red wine
salt and freshly ground black pepper

Rinse and dry the vine leaves and use the largest ones from the can or packet. Finely chop the onion and heat the oil in the wok. Add the onion and crush the garlic into the wok. Sprinkle in seasoning to taste and fry until the onion is soft but not browned. Add the lamb and fry this, breaking up the meat as it cooks, until well browned.

Stir in the marjoram and remove the meat mixture from the wok; set it aside to cool. There is no need to rinse the wok. When the mixture cools, use it to stuff the vine leaves. Place a small spoonful of the filling in the middle of a vine leaf. Fold the sides of the leaf over the meat, then fold the stalk end in towards the middle. Neatly roll the leaf from the stalk end, enclosing the filling in the folds and making sure that the package is secure. Place the leaf in the wok, with the folded side downwards. Continue until all the leaves and meat are used, laying them closely together in the wok and working from the centre outwards in a single layer.

When all the leaves are neatly arranged in the wok, mix the ingredients for the sauce, adding seasoning to taste. Stir until the tomato purée has dissolved and pour the mixture gently into the wok. Make sure that the sauce does not disturb the leaves and allow time for it to seep between the packages. Heat gently until the sauce simmers, then put the lid on the wok and keep the liquid simmering away gently for an hour. By this time the leaves should be tender – test one with a fork or knife.

Serve the dolmades, hot, straight from the wok, or if you wish to serve them cold, transfer them to a serving dish to cool, then chill thoroughly in the refrigerator. SERVES 6

**Note**  You can use fresh vine leaves if you like, but they will need to be simmered in salted water for 10 to 15 minutes before you can stuff them. This can be done in the wok, then the pan should be dried and lightly oiled before the filling is cooked.

# Stuffed Peppers

*When the peppers are cooked in steam there is no need to parboil them first. Serve these peppers with boiled rice – this can be cooked in the water which steams the peppers if you like. Simply add the rice to the water in the wok 15 minutes before the peppers are cooked. Remember to add a little salt and check that the rice does not dry up during cooking.*

4 red or green peppers
1 large onion
4 canned pineapple rings
2 sticks celery
75 g/3 oz roasted cashew nuts
2 cloves garlic

1 tablespoon oil
350 g/12 oz lean minced pork
salt and freshly ground black pepper
2 tablespoons chopped parsley

Try and choose squat, flat-based peppers that will stand up on their own for this recipe. Cut off and reserve the stalk ends of the peppers and scoop out all the seeds and pith inside. Chop the onion, cut the pineapple into small pieces and chop the celery and nuts. Crush the garlic and add this to the wok with the oil. Heat the oil, then add the onion and celery and cook until the onion is soft but not browned. Add the meat and stir-fry until well browned, breaking up the mince as it cooks. Stir in the pineapple, nuts and seasoning to taste, then add the chopped parsley and remove the wok from the heat or turn the heat off completely if it is gas.

Divide the meat filling between the peppers, pressing it well in, and place the stalk caps back on top. Wipe out the wok and place the steaming rack in the base. Stand the peppers in a heatproof dish and place this on the rack. Cover loosely with a piece of greased foil, fill the wok with water as far as the base of the dish, then bring to the boil. Cover the wok and steam the peppers for 25 to 30 minutes, then serve immediately. SERVES 4

# Lamb-stuffed Aubergines

*These stuffed aubergines are particularly moist and tender. Serve them with rice and a mixed salad — try adding cubes of feta cheese and some olives to a simple green salad for variety.*

2 large aubergines
salt and freshly ground black pepper
2 small onions
1 clove garlic
1 tablespoon olive oil
450 g/1 lb lean minced lamb
1 tablespoon concentrated tomato purée

3 tablespoons natural yogurt
4 slices mozzarella cheese
4 tablespoons roasted sesame seeds
GARNISH
1 tomato
parsley sprigs

Cut the aubergines in half lengthways and cut out most of the flesh, leaving an even layer behind in the skin. Chop the aubergine flesh and place it in a colander or sieve, sprinkle with salt and set aside over a plate or bowl. Chop the onions and garlic. When the aubergines have soaked in the salt for about 15 minutes, drain the flesh thoroughly and dry it on absorbent kitchen paper.

Heat the oil in the wok and add the minced lamb. Fry the meat over high heat, breaking it up with a wooden spoon or spatula, until well browned. Push the meat to one side of the wok and add the onion and garlic, season with salt and freshly ground black pepper and cook until soft but not browned. Now add the aubergine flesh to the wok and cook until it is soft, then stir all the ingredients in the wok together and cook for a few seconds. Transfer the mixture from the wok to a large mixing bowl and stir in the tomato purée and yogurt. Divide this stuffing between the aubergine shells, pressing it well in, and arrange the aubergines neatly in a heatproof serving dish. If the vegetables are likely to fall over as they cook, or if they are not quite close together, support them with a little crumpled foil. Place a slice of cheese on each aubergine half and sprinkle the sesame seeds over. Wipe out the wok with absorbent kitchen paper and place the steaming rack in the base. Pour in enough water to come up to the level of the rack and stand the dish on top. Bring to the boil, uncovered, then put the lid on the wok and steam for 20 to 25 minutes, or until the aubergines are very tender.

While the aubergines are cooking, slice the tomato and cut the slices in half. Garnish the cooked aubergines with the halved tomato slices and small sprigs of parsley, then serve immediately. SERVES 2 to 4

# Pipérade

*Illustrated on page 120*

*This is a dish of fried peppers and onions with scrambled eggs – it is ideal for a quick lunch or supper dish, or it can be served as a first course. Crisp bread and butter – French or Granary – is the best accompaniment.*

| | |
|---|---|
| 2 green peppers | 50 g/2 oz butter |
| 2 red peppers | 4 large eggs |
| 2 onions | salt and freshly ground black |
| 1 large clove garlic | pepper |

Cut off and discard the stalk ends of the peppers and remove all the seeds and pith from inside. Slice the pepper shells into very thin rings. Slice the onions thinly and separate the slices into rings. Crush the garlic into the wok and add the butter. Melt over a medium heat, then add the peppers and onions and fry fairly slowly until they are well cooked and soft.

Whisk the eggs with plenty of seasoning and add them to the wok, stirring well. Cook, stirring all the time, until the eggs are just beginning to set, then stop stirring and continue cooking over a low heat until the eggs are set to taste – they should be creamy rather than solid. Serve immediately, straight from the wok if you like. SERVES 4

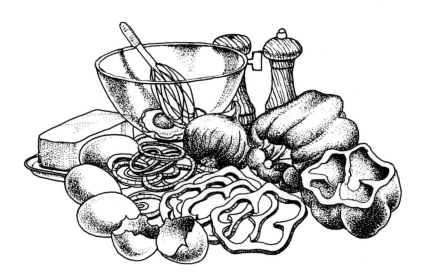

# Rice and Noodles

*Rice is an enormously useful ingredient to keep in the cupboard; seasoned and flavoured in all sorts of ways, it can be turned into a variety of dishes from the plainest to the most elaborate, and it's filling too!*
*Lots of these dishes are ideal for cooking in the wok – they are what I like to think of as my 'throw it all into the pan' type of meal. Easy to prepare and simple to serve, many of the recipes can be multiplied for serving to small gatherings of friends. Take the wok to the table and invest in an attractive, large serving spoon to scoop the paella, pullao, risotto or pilaf on to the plates. Bowls and chopsticks are also ideal for eating rice dishes, and not just the oriental ones – I find that a bowl and chopsticks seems to create far less washing-up than plates and cutlery!*
*There are a few dishes made with Chinese noodles – the wok is not really suitable for boiling other types of pasta, but you can of course try it if it is your only cooking pan.*

# Steamed Rice

350 g/12 oz long-grain rice (not　　　3 tablespoons water
　　the easy-cook variety)

Place the rice in a sieve and rinse it thoroughly under cold running water, then place it in a heatproof bowl or basin with the 3 tablespoons water. Place the steaming rack or bamboo steamer in the wok and fill the wok with water up to the level of the rack or steamer. Stand the basin of rice on the rack or in the steamer and put the lid of the wok on. Bring to the boil, then boil steadily for 45 minutes. Check occasionally during cooking to make sure that the water has not dried up.

Fork up the rice lightly before serving and remember that, unlike boiled rice, it has not been seasoned. This is ideal for serving with rich Chinese sauces. SERVES 4

# Fried Rice

2 tablespoons oil
225 g/8 oz long-grain rice
600 ml/1 pint chicken or beef stock
salt

Heat the oil in the wok, add the rice and stir-fry until the grains are lightly browned and transparent. Turn off the heat and gradually pour in the stock – take care not to scald your hand in the burst of steam which rises when the stock hits the hot surface of the wok. Bring to the boil, reduce the heat and stir in a little salt if the stock was unseasoned. Put the lid on the wok and simmer for about 15 minutes, or until the rice has absorbed all the stock. Fluff up the grains with a fork and serve. SERVES 4

## Variations

Add chopped onion, deseeded and chopped red and green peppers, diced carrots and celery, chopped chillies or crushed garlic when you fry the rice. If you wish to add frozen peas, sweet corn or other frozen mixed vegetables, stir them into the rice 5 minutes before the end of the cooking time. Add chopped nuts or herbs when the rice is cooked.

# Kedgeree

*Illustrated on page 132*

*Traditionally served for breakfast, kedgeree also makes a delicious lunch or supper dish. Serve this rice and fish mixture straight from the wok and offer a fresh green salad and some Granary bread as the only accompaniments.*

| | |
|---|---|
| 1 large onion | 450 g/1 lb smoked haddock |
| 2 tablespoons oil | 4 hard-boiled eggs |
| 225 g/8 oz long-grain rice | 2 tablespoons chopped parsley |
| $\frac{1}{2}$ teaspoon turmeric | salt and freshly ground black |
| 600 ml/1 pint chicken stock | pepper |

Chop the onion. Heat the oil in the wok, add the onion and cook, stirring frequently, until soft but not browned. Add the rice and fry this for a few minutes, turning it in the oil until it is lightly browned. Stir in the turmeric and gradually add the stock. Take care not to burn yourself in the gush of steam which rises as the liquid first enters the wok.

Bring to the boil, then lower the heat slightly and put the lid on the wok. Simmer for 10 minutes. Lay the fish on top of the half-cooked rice, re-cover the wok and continue to cook for a further 10 minutes. Use a fish slice to lift the fish on to a plate, then flake the flesh and discard any bones and the skin.

Quarter the hard-boiled eggs and stir these into the wok with the fish. Sprinkle over the parsley and season with salt and plenty of black pepper. Toss lightly and serve immediately. SERVES 4

**Right** *top:* Lamb Pilaf (page 137); *bottom:* Jambalaya and Fruity Green Salad (page 134)
**Overleaf** *clockwise, from the top:* Crunchy Tofu (page 155) with sauce accompaniment on far right, Vegetable Risotto (page 144) with courgette salad, Falafal (page 158)

# Paella

*Illustrated opposite*

*The wok is ideal for cooking paella because small pans will not hold all the ingredients necessary for this dish. Serve the paella straight from the wok with a crisp, mixed green salad.*

350 g/12 oz lean boneless pork
1 large onion
2 tablespoons olive oil
4 chicken drumsticks
2 large cloves garlic
1 red pepper
1 green pepper
225 g/8 oz long-grain rice
$\frac{1}{4}$ teaspoon powdered saffron

salt and freshly ground black pepper
450 ml/$\frac{3}{4}$ pint chicken stock
150 ml/$\frac{1}{4}$ pint full-bodied red wine
225 g/8 oz peeled cooked prawns
225 g/8 oz cooked mussels (fresh, frozen or canned in brine, but not pickled)
225 g/8 oz frozen peas
cooked whole shellfish to garnish

Cut the pork into small cubes and chop the onion. Heat the oil in the wok, add the chicken drumsticks and brown them all over. Add the pork, onion and crushed garlic, cover the wok and cook for 15 minutes. Check occasionally to make sure that the pork is not sticking to the pan.

Meanwhile, cut off and discard the stalk ends of the peppers, remove their seeds and pith, then slice the flesh into neat rings. Add these to the meats in the wok together with the rice and saffron. Cook, stirring, for a few minutes, then add seasoning to taste and pour in the stock and wine. Bring to the boil, reduce the heat and put the lid on the wok. Simmer for a further 15 minutes, then add the prawns, mussels and peas; do not stir these into the rice but let them cook on top. Re-cover the wok and cook for 15 minutes more. Toss the ingredients lightly and serve immediately, garnished with cooked whole shellfish of your choice. SERVES 4

*Top:* Kedgeree (page 128); *bottom:* Paella (above)

# Jambalaya

*Illustrated on page 129*

*Jambalaya is a spicy mixture of meats (ham and chicken), prawns and rice, with peppers and chillies too. All the ingredients are cooked together, making this dish particularly easy to prepare and serve, and it's great fun to eat it straight from the wok. So give your guests small bowls, and keep the food hot by placing the wok over a plate warmer or on a fondue burner turned down very low. Make the Fruity Green Salad (right) and have some warm pita bread or crisp French bread around in case anyone is ravenous!*

450 g/1 lb gammon, in one piece
450 g/1 lb chicken meat
1 large onion
1 green pepper
1 red pepper
4 green chillies
50 g/2 oz butter
2 cloves garlic

salt and freshly ground black pepper
225 g/8 oz long-grain rice
$\frac{1}{2}$ teaspoon turmeric
600 ml/1 pint chicken stock
dash of Tabasco sauce
225 g/8 oz peeled cooked prawns
paprika

Cut the gammon into bite-sized cubes and cut the chicken into similar-sized pieces. Chop the onion and cut the stalk ends off the peppers. Remove all the seeds and pith from inside the peppers and chop the flesh. Cut the stalk ends off the chillies and remove all their seeds, then slice them thinly.

Melt the butter in the wok and crush the garlic into it. Add the gammon, chicken and salt and pepper to taste, then fry until browned on all sides. Add the onion, peppers and chillies and continue cooking until the onion has softened slightly. Stir in the rice and turmeric, reduce the heat, then pour in the stock and add the Tabasco. Stir well and bring to the boil, cover the wok and reduce the heat so that the jambalaya simmers gently. Cook for 10 minutes before adding the prawns, then cook for a further 5 to 10 minutes, or until the rice is cooked and most of the stock has been absorbed to leave a moist dish. Sprinkle with a little paprika before serving. SERVES 4

# Fruity Green Salad

*This combination of green salad vegetables and sliced fresh peaches tastes superb with the jambalaya. You can prepare the greens in advance, but don't peel the peaches more than an hour before the meal or they may discolour badly.*

1 endive or crisp lettuce (for example, iceberg or cos)
1 bunch spring onions
$\frac{1}{4}$ cucumber
2 sticks celery
4 ripe peaches

juice of 1 lemon
2 slices onion
4 tablespoons olive oil
1 teaspoon prepared mild mustard
salt and freshly ground black pepper

Wash and trim the endive or lettuce, separate it into leaves and drain thoroughly, then shred roughly. Place in a salad bowl. Trim and chop the spring onions, lightly peel and dice the cucumber and add both to the salad. Trim the celery and cut it lengthways into very fine strips, then into 5-cm/2-in lengths. Place in a bowl of iced water and leave for 15 minutes, then drain and dry on absorbent kitchen paper before sprinkling over the salad.

Place the peaches in a bowl and pour on boiling water to cover. Leave to stand for 1 minute, then drain and peel the fruit. Halve the peaches and remove their stones, then cut the flesh into slices and sprinkle the lemon juice over them. Add to the salad, with a few slices of onion if liked.

Mix the olive oil with the remaining lemon juice, mustard and seasoning to taste, then sprinkle this dressing over the salad and serve.

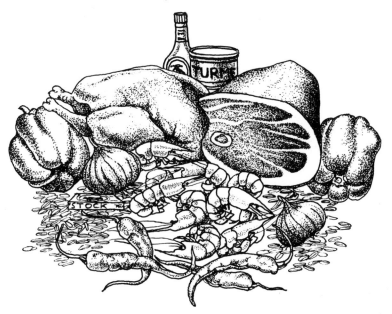

# Cashew Pilaf

*Serve a mayonnaise-dressed salad to complement this pilaf — why not try making coleslaw, for example? The combination of dried fruits, nuts and rice gives this dish an excellent flavour and texture and makes it ideal for serving as a meatless main dish.*

1 large onion
50 g/2 oz dried apricots
2 cloves garlic
2 tablespoons olive oil
1 stick cinnamon
bay leaf
2 cloves
225 g/8 oz long-grain rice
50 g/2 oz raisins

salt and freshly ground black pepper
600 ml/1 pint chicken or vegetable stock
1 (335-g/11.8-oz) can sweet corn
100 g/4 oz frozen peas
225 g/8 oz roasted cashew nuts
50 g/2 oz black olives
2 tablespoons chopped parsley

Chop the onion and apricots and crush the garlic cloves. Heat the oil in the wok and add the onion, garlic and broken cinnamon stick. Stir in the bay leaf and cloves and fry, stirring frequently, until the onion is soft but not browned. Add the rice and cook until the grains become transparent, then stir in the raisins and apricots, and season with plenty of freshly ground black pepper and a little salt. Pour in the stock and bring to the boil, then reduce the heat and simmer gently for 10 minutes.

Drain the sweet corn and add it to the rice mixture with the peas, cashews and olives. Do not stir these ingredients into the rice — just put the lid back on the wok and continue cooking for a further 5 to 10 minutes, by which time the rice should have absorbed most of the stock to leave a moist pilaf. Stir in the parsley and serve immediately. SERVES 4

# Lamb Pilaf

*Illustrated on page 129*

*This spicy dish of rice and lamb is simple to prepare and easy to serve straight from your wok, even if you're feeding a crowd of guests. Make a simple tomato salad sprinkled with finely sliced onion rings to complete the meal.*

675 g/1½ lb lean boneless lamb
1 large onion
1 large green pepper
2 tablespoons olive oil
25 g/1 oz flaked almonds
2 cloves garlic
225 g/8 oz long-grain rice
bay leaf
1 stick cinnamon

600 ml/1 pint robust red wine
50 g/2 oz black olives
salt and freshly ground black pepper
4 tablespoons chopped fresh coriander
GARNISH
1 lemon
paprika

Cut the lamb into neat, fairly small cubes and chop the onion. Cut the stalk end off the green pepper, then remove all the seeds and pith and chop the flesh. Heat the oil in the wok and add the flaked almonds. Cook until they are lightly browned, then remove them from the wok with a slotted spoon and drain on absorbent kitchen paper.

Add the lamb to the oil remaining in the wok and crush the garlic over it. Fry, turning frequently, until well browned on all sides. Add the onion, green pepper and rice and continue frying until the grains of rice are transparent and lightly browned. Add the bay leaf and cinnamon stick and carefully pour in the wine. Take care not to burn your arm in the gush of steam which rises as the wine hits the hot wok. Bring to the boil, put the lid on the wok and reduce the heat so that the pilaf simmers gently. Cook for 10 minutes.

While the pilaf is cooking, stone the olives and add these to the rice mixture after the 10 minutes' cooking time. Continue cooking for a further 5 minutes.

Cut the lemon for the garnish into eight wedges. When the pilaf is cooked, taste and adjust the seasoning if necessary, and stir in the coriander. To serve, arrange the lemon wedges around the rice, either in the wok or in a separate heated serving dish, and sprinkle a little paprika over each piece of lemon. Top with the fried almonds and serve. SERVES 4

# Fruit Pullao

*Illustrated on page 50*

*This is a particularly splendid pullao, with apricots, raisins and almonds added. To emphasise the scented basmati rice add a few drops of rose water.*

225 g/8 oz basmati rice
1 large onion
225 g/8 oz dried apricots
50 g/2 oz raisins
75 g/3 oz ghee (page 113) or butter
50 g/2 oz flaked almonds
2 sticks cinnamon
bay leaf
2 cloves
6 coriander seeds
2 green cardamoms
salt and freshly ground black pepper
600 ml/1 pint water

Rinse the rice thoroughly under plenty of cold running water, until the water runs clear, then set the rice aside to drain. Chop the onion and the apricots and mix both with the raisins.

Melt the ghee or butter in the wok and add the almonds. Fry until lightly browned, then remove with a slotted spoon. Add the onion mixture to the wok and fry over medium heat, stirring continuously, until the onion is just soft. Add the spices and continue cooking for a minute, then stir in salt and pepper to taste and the rice. Cook for another minute, then add the water. Bring to the boil and reduce the heat so that the rice barely simmers, then put the lid on the wok and cook for about 25 minutes. By this time all the liquid should have been absorbed and the rice should be cooked.

To serve, fork up the rice and sprinkle the almonds over the top. SERVES 4

# Paneer Pullao

*Spiced rice pullao is delicious, particularly when Indian cheese is stirred in as in this recipe. Basmati rice is best for making pullaos because it has a distinct, delicate flavour.*

225 g/8 oz basmati rice
600 ml/1 pint water
salt and freshly ground black pepper
1 large onion
50 g/2 oz ghee (page 113) or butter

1 stick cinnamon
4 cloves
bay leaf
2 green cardamoms
225 g/8 oz Paneer (page 156)

Rinse the basmati rice under plenty of cold water until the water runs clear, then drain. Place the rice in the wok and pour in the water. Add a little salt and bring to the boil, then reduce the heat so that the water just simmers and put the lid on the wok. Cook the rice for 25 minutes, then uncover the wok and transfer the rice to a bowl. While the rice is cooking, thinly slice the onion and separate the slices into rings.

Rinse the wok and grease it if necessary, then add the ghee or butter and melt it over a medium heat. Add the onion rings and fry until browned, then remove from the wok using a slotted spoon and drain on absorbent kitchen paper.

Add the spices to the fat remaining in the wok and cook gently for about 5 minutes. Add the cooked rice to the spices and carefully toss the grains in the fat – do not be too rough or you will break the grains and they will become stodgy. If there is not enough ghee or butter in the wok to coat the rice, then add a little more. Heat through gently for a minute. Meanwhile, cut the paneer into cubes, then stir them into the rice. When the pullao has heated through, sprinkle the fried onion rings over the top and serve immediately.
SERVES 4

**Note**   If you do not want to prepare the paneer, or if you do not have the time, full fat soft cheese can be cut into cubes and added to the pullao. The result is slightly different but equally delicious.

# Beef Risotto

*The wok is ideal for cooking dishes made up of lots of ingredients all simmered together. Risottos are easy to prepare, full flavoured and can be served straight from the wok. If you like you can offer a salad to accompany the risotto – try a simple courgette salad made from thinly sliced courgettes, dressed with olive oil, garlic and lemon juice, and garnished with plenty of chopped fresh basil or dill.*

| | |
|---|---|
| 1 stick celery | 4 tablespoons olive oil |
| 1 large onion | 450 g/1 lb lean minced beef |
| 100 g/4 oz carrots | 175 g/6 oz long-grain rice |
| 1 green pepper | salt and freshly ground black |
| 1 red pepper | pepper |
| 2 cloves garlic | 1 (397-g/14-oz) can tomatoes |
| 2 tablespoons concentrated tomato | 2 teaspoons dried oregano |
| purée | 4 tablespoons chopped parsley |
| 600 ml/1 pint hot beef stock | |

Chop the celery, onion and carrots. Cut off and discard the stalk ends of the peppers, remove the seeds and pith from inside and chop the flesh. Crush the garlic. Dissolve the tomato purée in the stock and set aside.

Heat the oil in the wok – take care not to overheat the oil or it will burn quickly. Add the beef to the oil and stir-fry until evenly browned, then push to one side of the wok. Gradually add the prepared vegetables and garlic and stir-fry them until they are just soft. Push these up the side of the wok to make room for the rice, then stir in the rice and cook it until the grains are transparent and slightly browned. Gradually stir all the ingredients in the wok together and season them with a little salt and pepper.

Carefully pour the stock mixture into the wok – a cloud of steam will rise from the hot fried ingredients so hold the jug to one side to avoid burning your arm. Add the tomatoes and oregano and bring to the boil. Put the lid on the wok and reduce the heat so that the risotto simmers gently. Cook for 15 minutes, by which time the rice should have absorbed most of the stock to leave a moist mixture. Stir in the parsley and fluff up the grains of rice with a fork. Serve immediately, straight from the wok if you like. SERVES 4

Wok Pizza (page 152) and variations. *Top:* Bacon Pizza; *centre, left to right:* Wok Pizza, Seafood Pizza, Salami Pizza; *bottom:* Pepper Pizza

# Egg-fried Rice with Sausage

*Chinese sausages are dried, spiced pork sausages containing pieces of meat and, sometimes, liver. They have a slightly sweet taste and should be cooked in moist dishes or steamed before being added to vegetable dishes. They are delicious and add an excellent flavour to steamed rice if they are balanced over the dish in which the rice is cooked, and then sliced diagonally to serve. Serve this rice dish with simple stir-fried meat and vegetables, or serve it just on its own because it is quite substantial and well flavoured.*

2 tablespoons oil
225 g/8 oz long-grain rice
4 large dried Chinese mushrooms
600 ml/1 pint chicken stock
8 Chinese sausages

1 bunch spring onions
2 eggs
1 (227-g/8-oz) can water
chestnuts

Heat half the oil in the wok and add the rice, then fry this until the grains are transparent and lightly browned. Meanwhile, place the mushrooms in a small basin and cover with boiling water. Allow to soak for 5 minutes.

When the rice is browned, carefully pour the stock into the wok. As the liquid hits the hot pan clouds of steam will rise, so take care not to burn your arm. When the steam has subsided, stand the steaming rack in the wok over the rice and place the sausages on this rack. Bring the stock back to the boil, then reduce the heat so that it simmers steadily. Drain the mushrooms and stand them on the rack next to the sausages. Put the lid on the wok and simmer for 15 minutes, or until the rice has absorbed all the stock.

Meanwhile, trim the spring onions and cut them diagonally into strips. Lightly beat the eggs and set aside. Drain and slice the water chestnuts.

When the rice is cooked, remove the steaming rack from the wok and slice the sausages diagonally. Slice the mushrooms and add these to the sausages, set aside and keep hot. Push the rice up the sides of the wok to make a well in the middle. Add the remaining oil to this space and fry the sliced water chestnuts for a minute, then remove them with a slotted spoon and add them to the sausages and mushrooms. Pour the egg into the wok and cook, stirring, until just beginning to set. Mix with the rice and cook for a few seconds.

Remove the wok from the heat and arrange the sausage mixture on top. Sprinkle the spring onions over and serve immediately. Alternatively, the rice mixture can be transferred to a serving dish and the sausage mixture added as above. SERVES 4

*Top:* Popcorn (page 161) and variations; *bottom:* Samosas (page 163)

# Vegetable Risotto

*Illustrated on page 130*

*This is a good dish to serve as a vegetarian main meal: make a creamy-dressed salad as an accompaniment – try some of the suggestions given below if you are stuck for ideas.*

4 sticks celery
1 green pepper
100 g/4 oz carrots
2 large onions
2 tablespoons olive oil
2 cloves garlic
225 g/8 oz walnut pieces
175 g/6 oz long-grain rice
salt and freshly ground black pepper

600 ml/1 pint chicken or vegetable stock
450 g/1 lb tomatoes
100 g/4 oz black olives
100 g/4 oz sweet corn
100 g/4 oz frozen peas
4 tablespoons chopped fresh herbs (for example, parsley, marjoram, basil, lemon balm, a little thyme and a little rosemary)

Slice the celery. Cut off and discard the stalk end of the pepper and remove all the seeds and pith from the inside, then roughly chop the flesh. Slice the carrots and roughly chop the onions.

Heat the oil in the wok, crush the garlic into it and add the walnuts. Fry, stirring frequently, until the nuts are lightly browned, then remove them from the wok using a slotted spoon and drain on absorbent kitchen paper. Add the prepared vegetables to the oil remaining in the wok and cook until slightly softened. Stir in the rice and seasoning to taste, then pour in the stock and bring to the boil. Put the lid on the wok and reduce the heat so that the risotto simmers gently. Cook for 10 minutes.

While the rice is cooking, place the tomatoes in a bowl and pour on enough boiling water to cover them completely. Leave to stand for 30 seconds to a minute, then drain, peel and quarter the tomatoes. Stone the olives and mix them with the tomatoes.

When the rice has cooked for 10 minutes, stir in the sweet corn and peas, place the tomatoes and olives on top (do not stir them in) and put the lid back on the wok. Continue simmering the risotto for a further 5 minutes, by which time all the stock should have been absorbed and the rice should be cooked. Before serving, stir in the tomatoes, olives, nuts and herbs. Serve straight from the wok if you like, with a creamy salad. SERVES 4

### Salad Suggestions

Serve beetroot slices dressed with soured cream which has been flavoured with a little orange rind and juice. Alternatively, thinly slice courgettes and dress them with a little single cream which has been seasoned with salt, freshly ground black pepper and a little freshly grated nutmeg. If you like, add a little mild mustard and chopped parsley too.

A crunchy bacon and spinach salad would also taste exciting with this risotto – shred washed and dried fresh spinach and place it in a bowl. Top with chopped spring onions, plenty of crisply fried bacon and croûtons, then make a dressing of mayonnaise with a little tomato purée and lemon juice, to pour over at the last minute.

# Prawn Fried Rice

*Illustrated on page 90*

*Fried rice is quite easy to prepare but it is important first to cook the rice sufficiently in the oil until the grains are transparent; that way the finished dish will always have a good flavour.*

| | |
|---|---|
| 1 onion | salt and freshly ground black |
| 3 tablespoons oil | pepper |
| 1 clove garlic | 600 ml/1 pint chicken stock |
| 225 g/8 oz long-grain rice | 225 g/8 oz frozen peas |
| | 225 g/8 oz peeled cooked prawns |

Chop the onion. Heat the oil in the wok and crush the garlic into it. Add the onion and cook until softened but not brown. Add the rice and stir-fry until the grains are transparent and lightly browned. Add seasoning to taste and carefully pour in the stock – take care because a cloud of steam will rise from the wok and this may burn your hand or arm if it is in the way. Bring to the boil, reduce the heat and put the lid on the wok, then simmer gently for 15 minutes.

When the rice has absorbed most of the stock, stir in the peas and prawns and continue cooking for a further 5 minutes; make sure that the rice does not overcook and burn at this stage. Serve straight from the wok or spoon the fried rice into a heated serving bowl. SERVES 4

# Noodles with Cucumber

*Stir-fried cucumber tastes very good, particularly with garlic-flavoured noodles. Serve these noodles with meat or fish dishes. Extra ingredients can also be added to make this a main dish and suggestions for these are given below.*

350 g/12 oz chow mein noodles
(thin Chinese egg noodles)
1.15 litres/2 pints boiling water
pinch of salt
½ cucumber

3 green chillies
1 bunch spring onions
2 tablespoons oil
1 clove garlic

Place the noodles in the wok and pour the boiling water over them. Add a pinch of salt and bring to the boil, then put the lid on the wok and reduce the heat so that the water simmers rapidly. Cook for 3 to 5 minutes, depending on the type of noodle. Check to see if the noodles are cooked after 3 minutes; when ready, they should be tender but not sticky.

While the noodles are cooking, finely peel the cucumber and cut it into matchstick strips. Cut the tops off the chillies and remove their seeds, then finely slice the green part. Trim and chop the spring onions.

Drain the noodles when they are cooked and heat the oil in the wok. Add the cucumber, chillies and spring onions and cook, stirring, for a minute. Crush the garlic into the wok and stir for another minute, then add the cooked noodles. Toss well to combine the ingredients and put the lid on the wok. Cook over gentle heat for 2 to 3 minutes, or until the noodles are hot. Serve immediately. SERVES 4

# Variations

This simple accompaniment can be turned into an interesting main dish by adding any of the following ingredients.

### Noodles with Prawns and Ham
Add 225 g/8 oz peeled cooked prawns and 225 g/8 oz shredded cooked ham to the noodles when they are returned to the wok for reheating.

### Spicy Chicken with Noodles
Cook 450 g/1 lb shredded chicken breast and 25 g/1 oz grated fresh root ginger in the oil in the wok before adding the cucumber and other vegetables.

### Noodles with Pork and Water Chestnuts
Finely shred 225 g/8 oz lean pork and fry this in the oil in the wok before adding the cucumber and other vegetables. Add 1 (227-g/8-oz) can water chestnuts, drained and sliced, with the cucumber. If you like, sprinkle a few roasted sesame seeds over before serving.

# Beef Chow Mein

*This dish makes a satisfying meal in itself; serve a cucumber and chicory salad as the only accompaniment.*

| | |
|---|---|
| 450 g/1 lb frying steak | salt |
| 1 small onion | 350 g/12 oz chow mein noodles |
| 1 stick celery | (thin Chinese egg noodles) |
| 4 large dried Chinese mushrooms | 2 tablespoons light sesame oil |
| 1 large clove garlic | 150 ml/$\frac{1}{4}$ pint beef stock |
| 2 tablespoons soy sauce | 4 tablespoons dry sherry |

Cut the meat into fine strips. Halve and thinly slice the onion and cut the celery into short, fine strips. Place the mushrooms in a small basin and cover with boiling water, then leave to stand for about 15 minutes, or until they are soft enough to slice. Crush the garlic and mix it with the soy sauce, then pour this over the meat in a basin and use your fingers to rub the sauce well into the strips of meat. Set aside.

Bring 1.15 litres/2 pints water to the boil in the wok and season it lightly with a little salt. Add the noodles and put the lid on the wok, then simmer for 5 minutes. Drain and set aside the noodles and wipe out the wok with absorbent kitchen paper. Drain and slice the mushrooms.

Heat the oil in the wok, add the steak and stir-fry for about 5 minutes, or until the meat is browned. Then add the onion and celery and cook for a minute. Stir in the mushrooms, stock and sherry and bring to the boil, then add the cooked noodles and toss them with the other ingredients. Cook for 2 to 3 minutes, then serve. SERVES 4

# Crispy Noodles
# with Mushrooms and Ham

*These crunchy noodles are delicious with stir-fried cooked ham and soaked Chinese mushrooms. You can boil the noodles in advance if you wish, ready for frying at the last minute.*

salt and freshly ground black
pepper
350 g/12 oz chow mein noodles
(thin Chinese egg noodles)
6 large dried Chinese mushrooms

225 g/8 oz cooked ham
1 bunch spring onions
2 tablespoons oil
50 g/2 oz butter

Pour 1.15 litres/2 pints water into the wok and add a little salt, then bring to the boil and add the noodles. Put the lid on the wok and simmer for about 5 minutes; when cooked the noodles should be tender but not sticky. Drain the noodles and place them on a plate, patting them into a round shape.

Place the mushrooms in a basin and pour in enough boiling water to cover them completely, then leave to soak for 15 minutes. Drain and slice. Cut the ham into shreds and trim and shred the spring onions.

Heat the oil and butter together in the wok and add the mushrooms, ham and spring onions. Cook for a few minutes, then remove with a slotted spoon and set aside. Slide the noodles into the wok and cook over a high heat until they are golden and crisp underneath, then turn them over and cook the second side in the same way. Sprinkle the ham mixture over the noodles and serve immediately. SERVES 4

# Side Dishes and Snacks

*This chapter includes a variety of recipes to go with all sorts of main dishes, and some to serve on their own for a light meal.*
*Indian breads are included — they cook very well in the wok — and there are a couple of fresh chutneys too. The advantage of having such a versatile cooking pan is that these small accompaniments can be cooked quickly before the main dish. The wok only needs a quick wipe before you can carry on preparing the rest of the menu.*
*There are a few interesting dishes which you could serve as a light main dish instead of meat or poultry — try Crunchy Tofu with its sauce accompaniment, for example, or the Falafal.*
*If you've never tried making a pizza in a pan, then now is the time to have a go. I have cooked quick pizza imitations in various frying pans, but never one which resembled the real thing. With my wok I can cook a light bread-based pizza with a crisp base and moist topping — it's delicious!*
*I found that this chapter was fun to test and I hope you will enjoy preparing these accompaniments to complete your meal.*

# Parathas

*These Indian breads are roughly triangular in shape and unleavened. Enriched with ghee and layered in texture, parathas are delicious with moist, spicy dishes.*

| | |
|---|---|
| 225 g/8 oz wholemeal flour | about 150 ml/$\frac{1}{4}$ pint water |
| $\frac{3}{4}$ teaspoon salt | 75 g/3 oz ghee (page 113) or butter |
| 2 tablespoons oil | extra ghee or butter for cooking |

Sift the flour and salt into a mixing bowl and discard the bran which is left in the sieve. Make a well in the flour and pour in the oil and water, then mix in the flour to make a firm dough. Knead thoroughly until smooth, then divide the dough into six equal portions.

Roll each piece of dough into a circle measuring about 15 cm/6 in. in diameter. Spread a little ghee or butter over the dough, leaving the edges free, and fold in half. Spread more ghee or butter over the semicircle of dough, again avoiding the very edge, and fold in half again to make a wedge shape. Pinch the edges of the dough together and roll out lightly into a triangular shape; the sides of the triangle should measure about 15 cm/6 in.

Melt a little ghee or butter in the wok and roll the pan to spread it round the sides. Place three parathas in the wok and cook until browned on the underside, turning the bread round once to make sure that it cooks evenly. Brush a little ghee or butter on top of the bread, turn it over and cook the second side until lightly browned. Again brush the top with a little ghee or butter and turn once more. Cook for 2 to 3 minutes over a medium heat, then serve immediately, in a napkin-lined basket. MAKES 6

## Variations

You can make this layered bread even more interesting by adding small amounts of ingredients when folding the bread. For example, add a little chopped and fried onion and chillies, mixed together, to both folds of the bread. Pinch the edges well together to seal in the filling and continue as above.

Lightly roasted poppy seeds and a few pinches of garam masala can also be rolled into the bread, or try adding a few roasted sesame seeds.

If you are feeling very adventurous, mash about 100 g/4 oz of cooked peas with a few finely chopped chillies and a pinch of garam masala and spread this over the bread before folding. (Put this mixture in the first fold only.) It's quite delicious, particularly when served with dishes made from paneer (Indian cheese).

# Naan

*Illustrated on page 50*

*Naan bread is an Indian bread which is traditionally cooked in a tandoor, or Indian clay oven. The bread is leavened with yeast and it cooks very well on the sides of the wok, with the lid on for part of the cooking time.*

350 g/12 oz strong plain flour
$\frac{3}{4}$ teaspoon salt
2 teaspoons dried yeast
about 150 ml/$\frac{1}{4}$ pint lukewarm
water

2 teaspoons sugar
150 ml/$\frac{1}{4}$ pint natural yogurt
oil

Sift the flour and salt into a mixing bowl. Sprinkle the yeast over the water and stir in the sugar. Leave the yeast mixture in a warm place until frothy – this should take about 15 minutes, perhaps less if the room is warm.

Make a well in the centre of the flour and pour in the yeast liquid and yogurt. Gradually mix the flour into the liquid ingredients to make a soft dough. Knead the dough thoroughly on a well-floured work surface for about 10 minutes, or until it is very smooth and elastic. Set aside in a warm place, in an oiled bowl covered with cling film, until the dough has doubled in size. The length of time this takes will depend upon how warm the surroundings are – about an hour should be long enough in a room of average warmth.

When the dough has risen, turn it out on to a floured surface and knead it lightly, then divide it into three equal portions. Shape each portion roughly into an oval and then slap it from hand to hand to stretch the dough into an oval about 18 cm/7 in long and 7.5 to 10 cm/3 to 4 in wide.

Lay the shaped bread on a well-floured surface and heat the wok, having first greased it with a little oil. Get the wok very hot indeed, then lay the bread in it, resting the pieces on the sides. Cook over high heat until the bread in the middle of the wok has browned, then turn the ovals round so that the other ends are in the middle, and cook until they too are well browned. Turn the bread over and repeat for the second side. Reduce the heat and turn the bread over again, put the lid on the wok and cook very gently for 3 to 5 minutes, turning the bread once. Serve immediately, in a napkin-lined basket. MAKES 3

# Wok Pizza

*Illustrated on page 141*

*Here is a very quick and easy recipe for a pizza, and it's not a second rate attempt at imitating the real thing either! The base is made of bread mix, which is cooked on the hot surface of the wok to give a crisp light result similar to that achieved when a pizza is cooked in a very hot oven. The topping is moist and well flavoured, and there is a whole list of alternative topping suggestions given below.*

150 g/5 oz bread mix
about 100 ml/4 fl oz lukewarm
water
TOPPING
1 large onion
3 tablespoons olive oil
2 cloves garlic
1 teaspoon dried oregano
$\frac{1}{2}$ teaspoon dried thyme

1 teaspoon marjoram
salt and freshly ground black
pepper
4 tablespoons concentrated tomato
purée
175 g/6 oz mozzarella cheese
1 (50-g/1$\frac{3}{4}$-oz) can anchovies
a few black olives

The quantity of bread mix you need to use is about half of a standard packet size. Make it up with the water, having read the packet instructions first to check the quantities – for this recipe you have to add just a little extra water to give a soft dough. Knead the dough for about 10 minutes, again reading the instructions on the packet. Set aside while the topping is being prepared.

Finely chop the onion. Heat the oil in the wok and add the onion, then crush the garlic into it. Cook until soft but not browned, then add the herbs and seasoning and remove from the heat. Transfer the topping to a basin and stir in the tomato purée. Slice the cheese and halve the anchovy fillets, reserving the oil from the can to pour over the pizza if you like. Remove the stones from a few black olives.

Roll out the dough to give a 25-cm/10-in round. Heat the wok – it should still contain some oil from the filling, or at least it should be well greased. Carefully lift the pizza base into the wok; use a spatula to do this to make sure that there will be no creases in the dough. Reduce the heat so that the bread will not brown and cook for a few minutes, until the underside is starting to cook and form a crust. Turn the dough over and spread the tomato mixture on top. Lay the slices of cheese evenly over the pizza and arrange the anchovy fillets and olives in a lattice pattern on top.

Put the lid on the wok and increase the heat so that the base of the pizza cooks crisply and bubbles slightly. The pizza should be cooked through in about 5 minutes. During cooking, carefully lift the sides of the dough and make sure that it is not burning in the middle underneath. You can slide the pizza round the wok slightly to ensure that it cooks evenly. Serve immediately, sliding the pizza out on to a warmed serving platter and cutting it into portions if you wish to serve more than one. SERVES 1 TO 4

# Variations

Retain the tomato base and try any of the following topping ideas. The ingredients should be sprinkled over the tomato mixture before you put the cheese on top.

**Seafood Pizza**    Sprinkle over 100 g/4 oz peeled cooked prawns and add 1 (198-g/7-oz) can tuna fish, flaked with its oil.

**Salami Pizza**    Arrange 50 g/2 oz thinly sliced Italian salami over the tomato mixture. Omit the anchovies and use stuffed green olives, sliced, instead of the black ones.

**Pepper Pizza**    Sauté 2 thinly sliced red or green peppers in the oil and remove them from the wok before adding the onion and tomato mixture. Sprinkle the peppers over the tomato topping before adding the cheese. Omit the anchovies and top the pizza with 50 g/2 oz cooked ham, cut into fine strips, with the olives.

**Bacon Pizza**    Chop 175 g/6 oz rindless streaky bacon and fry it in the wok before preparing the tomato topping. Use only 50 g/2 oz mozzarella and cut it into small cubes. Mix the fried bacon with 1 (396-g/14-oz) can artichoke hearts, drained, and the anchovies and olives. Top the tomato mixture with the bacon mixture and dot the cubes of cheese over the top.

# Chinese-style Tofu

*Tofu, or bean curd, is made from ground, soaked soya beans – it is a sort of soya cheese. To eat on its own it is tasteless and has a texture which is reminiscent of a chilled custard, but it is high in food value (protein) and because it lacks any distinctive taste it can be seasoned and flavoured in any number of dishes. You can buy tofu in health food stores and Chinese supermarkets. Traditionally used in Chinese cooking, it is also used in lots of vegetarian dishes. Serve Chinese-style Tofu with spicy rice or meat dishes, or serve it on its own as a starter.*

1 (227-g/8-oz) can bamboo shoots
175 g/6 oz mangetout peas
350 g/12 oz tofu
4 tablespoons oil

1 clove garlic
4 tablespoons soy sauce
2 tablespoons roasted sesame seeds

Slice, then shred the drained bamboo shoots. Trim the ends of the mangetout peas and string them if necessary. Cut the tofu into 5-mm/$\frac{1}{4}$-in thick slices.

Heat the oil in the wok and crush the garlic into it. Add the tofu and fry the slices until crisp and golden, then remove them from the wok with a slotted spoon and drain on absorbent kitchen paper. Add the mangetout peas and bamboo shoots to the wok, and stir-fry for 5 minutes, then sprinkle the soy sauce and sesame seeds over them. Return the tofu to the wok and cook for a further minute before serving. SERVES 4

# Crunchy Tofu

*Illustrated on page 130*

*Soft, light tofu tastes delicious when coated in breadcrumbs and fried until crisp, then served with a tangy sauce. Serve this dish as a starter, or serve it as a main meal accompanied by salad, baked potatoes or a rice dish.*

450 g/1 lb tofu
4 tablespoons plain flour
freshly grated nutmeg
salt and freshly ground black pepper
1 egg
75–100 g/3–4 oz dry white breadcrumbs
900 ml/1½ pints oil for deep frying
SAUCE
1 large clove garlic

2 tablespoons concentrated tomato purée
4 tablespoons chopped fresh herbs
150 ml/¼ pint natural yogurt
150 ml/¼ pint double cream, lightly whipped
salt and freshly ground black pepper
GARNISH
watercress sprigs
lemon wedges

Cut the tofu into slices. Mix the flour with grated nutmeg to taste and plenty of salt and pepper, then use it to coat the tofu. Lightly beat the egg, then dip the slices of tofu in the beaten egg, coat them thoroughly in the breadcrumbs and chill.

To prepare the sauce, crush the garlic into the tomato purée in a small bowl, then stir in the herbs, yogurt, cream and seasoning to taste. Chill until required.

Pour the oil for deep frying into the wok and heat it to 190 C/375 F. Add the tofu and fry, a few pieces at a time, until crisp and golden. Remove with a slotted spoon and drain on absorbent kitchen paper. Keep hot.

When all the tofu is cooked, arrange the slices on a heated serving dish and garnish with watercress sprigs and lemon wedges. Serve immediately, with the sauce handed separately. SERVES 4

# Fresh Mint Chutney

*Unlike chutney preserves, fresh chutneys are prepared to complement a particular dish and are not for storing – they are side dishes which are commonly served with Indian foods. This tangy chutney goes very well with mild curries or spiced dishes and it can be prepared in the wok before the main dish is cooked; simply wipe out the wok when you transfer the chutney to its serving dish.*

450 g/1 lb onions
6 green chillies
50 g/2 oz ghee (page 113) or butter
salt and freshly ground black
pepper

1 tablespoon garam masala
4 tablespoons chopped mint
2 teaspoons sugar
2 tablespoons vinegar

Finely chop the onions. Cut the stalk ends off the chillies and remove all the seeds from inside, then chop the green parts finely and mix with the onions.

Melt the ghee or butter in the wok and add the onion mixture. Cook over a medium heat until the onion is soft, stirring frequently. Add salt and pepper to taste and the garam masala, then stir in the mint, sugar and vinegar. Continue cooking until the excess liquid has evaporated, then spoon the chutney into a small serving dish and set aside to cool. SERVES 4 to 6

# Paneer

*Paneer is Indian cheese. It is easy to make and it can be flavoured with herbs or spices for eating on its own, or it can be used plain in rice, vegetable and meat dishes. If you are preparing more than 225 g/8 oz it is probably easier to make it in two separate batches.*

1.15 litres/2 pints creamy milk            6 tablespoons lemon juice

Bring the milk to the boil in a saucepan. When the milk reaches boiling point, turn off the heat and whisk in the lemon juice; continue whisking until the milk curdles, then set it aside to cool.

When cold, strain the curds through a piece of muslin and hang them up until they are fairly dry, then squeeze the cheese out gently to remove all the excess moisture. Press the cheese into a small tin or dish and press it under a heavy weight in the refrigerator for 2 to 4 hours. MAKES 100 g/4 oz

# Fried Paneer

*This is absolutely delicious – if you like Indian food then you are sure to love this dish. Serve the cubes of paneer, neatly arranged in a small dish, with curried meat or poultry dishes, vegetables or rice. Served simply with a small amount of green salad ingredients and some Indian bread, it also makes an unusual first course. If you are planning to serve the paneer as part of a full Indian meal, then cook it in the wiped-out wok when you have made the main dish.*

450 g/1 lb Paneer (page 156)
4 tablespoons plain flour
salt and freshly ground black pepper
1 onion

4 green chillies
ghee (page 113) or oil for frying
2 tablespoons chopped fresh thyme
chilli powder (optional)
lemon wedges to garnish

Cut the prepared paneer into 2-cm/1-in cubes, coat with a little flour and sprinkle with salt and pepper, then set aside in the refrigerator while you prepare the remaining ingredients. Thinly slice the onion and separate the slices into rings. Cut the tops off the chillies and remove all their seeds, then slice the chillies finely.

Melt a little ghee or heat some oil in the wok and add the cubes of paneer. Fry on one side until golden brown, then turn over and fry the second side. Transfer to a heated serving dish using a slotted spoon and keep hot. Add the chillies to the fat remaining in the wok and cook quickly, then sprinkle them over the paneer. Add the onion rings to the wok and cook for just a minute, then sprinkle the thyme over them. Toss briefly before sprinkling them over the paneer. Top with just a little chilli powder, if you like, and serve immediately, garnished with lemon wedges. SERVES 4

# Falafal

*Illustrated on page 130*

*These crunchy chick pea balls, served with a salad and some warm pita bread, make a delicious light lunch or supper dish. They are also ideal for taking on picnics.*

225 g/8 oz dried chick peas
salt and freshly ground black
   pepper
$\frac{1}{2}$ teaspoon ground coriander
2 tablespoons chopped mixed
   parsley and thyme
2 cloves garlic
900 ml/1$\frac{1}{2}$ pints oil for deep frying
SALAD
1 crisp lettuce (for example,
   iceberg or cos)

1 small red onion
$\frac{1}{2}$ cucumber
100 g/4 oz black olives
4 tomatoes
DRESSING
50 g/2 oz crunchy peanut butter
4 tablespoons olive oil
grated rind and juice of 1 lemon
dash of Tabasco sauce
salt and freshly ground black
   pepper

Soak the chick peas overnight in cold water to cover. Next day, drain them and grind them finely in a liquidiser. Transfer the ground mixture to a bowl and stir in seasoning to taste, the coriander, herbs and crushed garlic. Mix the ingredients thoroughly, then take small spoonfuls of the mixture and shape into balls about the size of walnuts. Knead thoroughly to make the mixture bind together.

To make the salad, shred the lettuce and place it in a large bowl. Thinly slice the onion and divide the slices into rings, then thinly slice the cucumber. Mix both into the lettuce. Stone the olives and add them to the salad. Lastly, place the tomatoes in a large heatproof bowl and add boiling water to cover. Leave for 30 seconds to a minute, then drain and peel the tomatoes. Cut them into quarters or eighths and add them to the salad, then toss the salad lightly and arrange it on a serving platter. Mix all the ingredients for the dressing and add seasoning to taste. Pour the dressing over the salad.

Heat the oil for deep frying in the wok until it reaches 190 C/375 F, then add the chick pea balls, a few at a time, and fry until golden brown. Drain on absorbent kitchen paper and pile the hot falafal on top of the salad. Serve immediately, with plenty of warm pita bread. SERVES 4

*Top:* Pear and Plum Compote (page 173); *bottom:* Crème Caramel (page 170)

# Popcorn

*Illustrated on page 142*

*Making popcorn at home is great fun, but without a large pan with a lid you can end up with a load of corn popping all over the kitchen! The wok is ideal for making popcorn – the lid keeps all the corn in and the large surface area gives plenty of room for the corn to cook quickly. I was interested to see just how much corn I could pop in my wok and, to my amazement, I used 150 g/5 oz of uncooked corn – this quantity completely filled the wok! It took a great deal of butter and sugar to make it all sweet and sticky but it would be ideal for a large party; I off-loaded mine on to surprised neighbours!*

| | |
|---|---|
| 2 tablespoons oil | 75 g/3 oz butter |
| 50 g/2 oz popping corn | 50 g/2 oz sugar |

Heat the oil in the wok until it is just beginning to smoke. Slide in all the corn at once and put the lid on the wok straightaway. Using oven gloves to hold the wok and its lid, shake the pan occasionally and cook over a medium-high heat until the popping stops.

When the corn has stopped popping open the wok and add the butter, in knobs, then sprinkle in the sugar. Cool the popcorn, with the lid on and shaking the wok all the time, for 2 to 3 minutes. Open the wok and toss the corn in the buttery caramel, then turn the corn into a bowl and pour in any caramel from the wok. Leave for a minute or two because it will still be very hot, then serve. MAKES a 1.15-litre/2-pint bowlful

## Variations

The popcorn can also be served as a savoury snack. Cook it as above and when the corn has stopped popping sprinkle it with chopped spring onions, grated cheese, chopped ham, fried chopped bacon, butter with herbs and salt and pepper, or any other combination of ingredients which takes your fancy. Try having a popcorn party and cook the corn while your guests look on!

*Top:* Blackcurrant Pudding (page 167); *bottom:* Jam Roly-poly (page 169)

# Swiss Dumplings

*These are very tasty and satisfying, but not at all stodgy as you may at first think. Here they are served on a salad, but if you like you can serve them with hot vegetables – baked or roast potatoes, simmered cabbage or beans, or carrots and peas.*

100 g/4 oz self-raising flour
pinch of salt
1 teaspoon dried mixed herbs
50 g/2 oz shredded beef suet
4–6 tablespoons cold water
prepared mustard of your choice
(mild sweet Swedish mustard is
excellent)
4 slices good-quality cooked ham
4 slices Emmental cheese

ACCOMPANIMENT
4 sticks celery
1 bunch spring onions
2 courgettes
2 tablespoons olive oil
dash of lemon juice
salt and freshly ground black
pepper
1 small clove garlic

Sift the flour and salt into a mixing bowl and add the herbs and suet. Stir in sufficient water to make a soft dough, knead the dough lightly on a floured surface and divide it into four equal portions. Roll out each to give a rectangle measuring about 10 × 15 cm/4 × 6 in – this size is only a guide and it doesn't matter if the rectangle is smaller. Spread a little mustard to taste over the dough and fold the ham slices so that they will fit on the rectangles. Place the cheese on top, folding the slices if necessary. Dampen the edges of the dough and fold the rectangle in half, to completely enclose the ham and cheese. You should now have a rectangle which measures approximately 10 × 7.5 cm/4 × 3 in. Pinch the edges of the dough together to seal them and lay the dumplings on a sheet of buttered foil. Fold the edges of the foil firmly together to prevent any steam from entering and lay the package on the steaming rack in the wok. Pour in enough water to come up to the level of the rack without wetting the foil, then bring to the boil and put the lid on the wok. Boil for 30 minutes.

While the dumplings are cooking prepare the accompaniment. Trim the celery and cut it into fine strips. Cut the spring onions into similar-sized strips and do the same with the courgettes. Mix all these ingredients together in a basin and pour over the oil and lemon juice, then season to taste and crush the garlic over. Mix thoroughly before transferring to a serving platter.

When the dumplings are cooked arrange them on the salad and serve immediately. SERVES 4

# Samosas

*Illustrated on page 142*

*These are small Indian pasties filled with either meat or vegetables. They are meant to be a snack, but they are also ideal for serving as a starter or as one of the side dishes in an Indian meal.*

| | |
|---|---|
| 1 onion | salt and freshly ground black |
| 2 green chillies | pepper |
| 15 g/$\frac{1}{2}$ oz fresh root ginger | beaten egg |
| 1 tablespoon oil | DOUGH |
| 2 cloves garlic | 100 g/4 oz plain flour |
| $\frac{1}{2}$ teaspoon mustard seeds | pinch of salt |
| 225 g/8 oz lean minced beef | 1 egg |
| 2 tablespoons chopped fresh | 3 tablespoons oil |
| coriander leaves (optional) | 1 tablespoon water |

Finely chop the onion, deseed and chop the chillies and finely chop the ginger. Heat the oil in the wok and add the onion and ginger, then fry until the onion is soft but not browned. Stir in the chillies, crushed garlic, mustard seeds and beef, and cook, breaking up the meat as it cooks, until evenly browned. Add the coriander and seasoning to taste, then remove this filling from the wok and wipe out the pan.

To make the dough, sift the flour into a bowl with the salt. Make a well in the cente and add the lightly beaten egg, oil and water. Stir these ingredients together in the middle of the flour until they are lightly mixed, then gradually stir in the flour and knead together to make a firm dough. Knead thoroughly on a lightly floured board until very smooth, then divide the dough into eight evenly sized portions.

Roll out each portion of dough to give a round measuring about 15 cm/6 in. in diameter. Take a circle of dough in the palm of your hand and make a pleat in it to take up about a quarter of the circle. Lift the dough off the palm and hold it between your thumb and forefinger, with your thumb and forefinger formed into an almost closed circle; the pleated side of the dough should be over your thumb and the main part of the dough should hang down into your hand to form a cone. Spoon some of the mixture into the cone and brush the edges with a little beaten egg, then pinch the edges together firmly, to seal in the filling. When the samosa is laid flat it should now be almost triangular in shape. Repeat with the remaining dough and filling.

Wipe out the wok and pour in the oil for deep frying. Heat the oil to 190 C/375 F and fry the samosas, one or two at a time, until they are crisp and golden. Drain on absorbent kitchen paper and serve hot or cold. MAKES 8

# Fresh Mango Relish

*Illustrated on page 39*

*Serve this sweet fruit relish with hot curries or spiced dishes. It's also very good with barbecued food, or with simple fried chops and steaks.*

2 mangoes (choose ones which are
only just ripe)
2 onions
75 g/3 oz butter
3 cloves garlic

salt and freshly ground black
pepper
2 tablespoons vinegar
2 teaspoons sugar
2 cloves
1 stick cinnamon

Using a sharp pointed knife, cut round the mangoes lengthways, in as far as the large stone, then carefully cut between the stone and the flesh to remove all the fruit in two portions. Peel and slice the mango flesh. Finely chop the onions.

Melt the butter in the wok and crush the garlic into the butter. Add the onions and fry, stirring frequently, until soft but not browned. Add salt and pepper to taste, and the vinegar, sugar and spices, and stir in the sliced mangoes. Bring to the boil and simmer gently for 10 minutes, then transfer to a serving dish and allow to cool. SERVES 4

# Puddings

*I'm sure you never anticipated cooking puddings in your wok when you first rushed out and bought it, but that's not to say you will be disappointed with the results. Here is a limited selection of puddings which can be cooked to advantage in the wok.*

*The steaming rack is used as a stand for steamed puddings – those old favourites which you may not have prepared for years, or even never before if you don't have a huge saucepan and steamer. In your wok, these puddings will cook perfectly.*

*Fruit fritters also cook very well in the wok, as do compotes. There is even a recipe for crème caramel, just in case your wok really is your main cooking pan in a bedsit kitchen.*

*I think this chapter really does emphasise the versatility of the wok, and I hope you'll agree when you've tried some of these recipes.*

# Upside-down Pudding

*The wok is very useful for steaming sweet puddings, and here is an impressive yet economical dessert for cool winter days. Serve this pudding with a custard sauce or whipped cream.*

4 canned pineapple rings
6 glacé cherries
100 g/4 oz butter
100 g/4 oz caster sugar

grated rind of 1 large orange
2 eggs
100 g/4 oz self-raising flour

Arrange three of the pineapple rings in the base of a buttered 15-cm/6-in soufflé dish. Cut the remaining pineapple ring into thirds and arrange the pieces between the rings in the dish. Place the cherries in any gaps between the rings and place one in the centre.

Cream the butter with the sugar and orange rind until pale and soft. Gradually beat in the eggs with just a little of the flour, then use a metal spoon to fold in the remaining flour. Spoon the mixture into the dish, taking care not to disturb the arrangement of the fruit in the base. Wrap the dish completely in foil, making sure that it is securely folded to prevent any steam from entering. Stand the dish on the steaming rack in the wok and pour in enough water to come up to the base of the dish. Put the lid on the wok and bring the water to the boil, then boil steadily for $1\frac{1}{2}$ hours. Check to make sure that the wok does not boil dry during cooking and add more boiling water if necessary.

When cooked, carefully lift the dish from the wok and remove the foil wrapping, then turn the pudding out on to a heated serving plate and serve hot. SERVES 6

# Blackcurrant Pudding

*Illustrated on page 160*

*This recipe is excellent for turning a small quantity of blackcurrants into a deliciously well-flavoured pudding. Serve it with whipped cream or vanilla ice cream.*

| | |
|---|---|
| 450 g/1 lb fresh or frozen blackcurrants | 2 eggs |
| 100 g/4 oz butter or margarine | 175 g/6 oz self-raising flour |
| 175 g//6 oz caster sugar | 1 teaspoon baking powder |
| | caster sugar to decorate (optional) |

Top and tail fresh blackcurrants, rinse and drain them and set aside; do not defrost frozen fruit. Cream the butter or margarine with the sugar until very soft and pale, then gradually beat in the eggs. Sift the flour and baking powder together, then gently fold into the pudding mixture using a metal spoon.

Place about one-third of the blackcurrants in the base of a deep buttered 15-cm/6-in soufflé dish. Fold the remaining fruit into the pudding mixture and spoon this over the currants in the dish. Spread the mixture evenly and wrap the whole dish in plenty of foil, making sure that it is sharply folded to seal all the edges and prevent any steam from entering and making the pudding soggy during cooking.

Place the steaming rack in the wok and pour in enough water to come up to the top of it. Stand the dish on the rack and bring the water to the boil. Put the lid on the wok and boil steadily for about 2 hours. Check to make sure that the liquid does not boil dry during the cooking time and top it up with more boiling water if necessary.

To serve, lift the dish from the wok and remove the foil, then turn the pudding out on to a heated serving dish. Sprinkle with a little caster sugar before serving, if liked. SERVES 6

# Tipsy Coffee Ring
# with Mocha Sauce

*This is definitely not the pudding for anyone who is trying to diet – it is so tempting! Serve it for a special winter pudding and if you want to go really mad, offer clotted cream as well as the mocha sauce.*

150 ml/¼ pint strong fresh black coffee
75 g/3 oz butter
75 g/3 oz caster sugar
75 g/3 oz self-raising flour
75 g/3 oz ground almonds
1 teaspoon baking powder
1 large egg

MOCHA SAUCE
2 tablespoons caster sugar
50 ml/2 fl oz strong fresh black coffee
225 g/8 oz plain chocolate
50 g/2 oz butter
4 tablespoons Tia Maria

Make the coffee from a strong continental roast and set it aside to cool. Meanwhile, cream the butter with the sugar until very soft and pale. Sift the flour into a bowl and mix in the ground almonds and baking powder. Lightly beat the egg and mix this into the creamed mixture.

Gradually mix the dry ingredients and the coffee into the creamed mixture, alternating the two to give a soft dropping consistency. Thoroughly grease a 1.15-litre/2-pint ring mould and spoon the pudding mixture into it. Wrap the whole of the ring mould in plenty of foil and fold the edges firmly to make sure that no steam enters during cooking. Place the steaming rack in the wok and stand the mould on it. Pour in enough water to come up as far as the tin and bring to the boil. Put the lid on the wok and boil steadily for 1½ hours. Check to make sure that the water does not boil dry during cooking and top it up with more boiling water if necessary.

Towards the end of the cooking time for the pudding, prepare the mocha sauce. Dissolve the sugar in the coffee and set aside. Melt the chocolate with the butter in a basin over a saucepan of hot water. Slowly trickle the coffee syrup into the melted ingredients, stirring continuously. Stir in the Tia Maria and keep the sauce hot.

To serve, lift the mould out of the wok and remove the foil wrapping. Turn the pudding out on to a heated serving dish and spoon just a little of the mocha sauce over. Serve the remaining sauce in a separate sauceboat.
SERVES 6

# Jam Roly-poly

*Illustrated on page 160*

*This is an economical winter pudding for hungry people. Serve it with a custard sauce.*

225 g/8 oz self-raising flour
100 g/4 oz shredded beef suet
pinch of salt

scant 150 ml/$\frac{1}{4}$ pint water
350 g/12 oz strawberry jam
caster sugar to decorate

Sift the flour into a mixing bowl and add the suet and salt. Stir in sufficient water to make a soft dough, then knead it very lightly and roll it out on a floured surface to give a rectangle measuring about 25 × 20 cm/10 × 8 in. Spread the jam over the centre of the dough, leaving a 1-cm/$\frac{1}{2}$-in border all round the edge. Fold this dough border over the jam, brush the edges with a little water, then roll up the dough to enclose the jam. Place the roly-poly on a large piece of greased foil and wrap it up, sealing the edges thoroughly to make sure that no steam enters during cooking.

Place the steaming rack in the wok and lay the package on it. Pour in enough water to come up to the rack without touching the foil. Bring the water to the boil, cover the wok and simmer for 1$\frac{1}{2}$ hours, adding more water as necessary.

To serve, open the foil, slide the roly-poly on to a warm serving plate and sprinkle it with a little caster sugar. Serve immediately. SERVES 4

# Caramelised Pineapple

*The wok is ideal for cooking this simple dessert because there is enough room to cook all the sliced fruit together. Serve with whipped cream or good-quality vanilla ice cream.*

1 large pineapple
50 g/2 oz butter
4 tablespoons demerara sugar
4 tablespoons kirsch

2 tablespoons chopped pistachio nuts
2 tablespoons chopped maraschino cherries

Trim the leaves off the pineapple and cut off the stalk end. Using a sharp knife, cut off all the peel and remove the spines. Slice the fruit fairly thickly and remove the hard core from each slice.

Melt the butter in the wok and add the pineapple slices, frying both sides for a few seconds. Sprinkle the sugar over and turn the slices of fruit, then cook until the sugar caramelises, turning the fruit once again. As soon as the sugar is lightly browned, turn off the heat and pour in the kirsch. Sprinkle on the nuts and cherries and serve. SERVES 4

# Crème Caramel

*Illustrated on page 159*

*Make these individual custards the day before you plan to serve them and chill them thoroughly overnight. Although the caramel has to be prepared in a saucepan, steaming the custards in the wok saves putting the oven on, and they are less likely to curdle cooked this way.*

| | |
|---|---|
| 100 g/4 oz sugar | 2 scant tablespoons sugar |
| 100 ml/4 fl oz water | 350 ml/12 fl oz milk |
| 2 small eggs | vanilla pod |

Place the 100 g/4 oz of sugar and the water in a saucepan and bring to the boil, stirring occasionally until the sugar dissolves. Boil hard, without stirring at all, until the syrup caramelises – this should take 3 or 4 minutes. As soon as the syrup starts to change colour watch it very carefully, then when it is a light caramel colour remove the pan from the heat and roll the syrup round the sides of the saucepan – it will continue cooking in the heat of the pan. When it becomes a dark caramel colour divide it between four ovenproof ramekin dishes and roll the caramel round the sides of each. Hold the dishes with a tea towel as you do this because they become very hot. Set aside.

Whisk the eggs with the tablespoons of sugar – I find 1 tablespoon of sugar is just too little and, for my liking, 2 tablespoons gives a custard that is just too sweet, so adjust the quantity to taste.

Pour the milk into a saucepan and add the broken vanilla pod, then bring the milk to the boil and set it aside to cool until hand hot. Remove the vanilla pod and pour the milk on to the eggs, whisk lightly, then strain the custard into the ramekins. Cover each with a square of buttered foil, pinching the edge firmly under the rim of the dish to prevent steam from entering. Stand the dishes on the steaming rack in the wok and pour in enough water to come up to the level of the rack. Bring the water to the boil, then reduce the heat so that the water simmers and put the lid on the wok. Simmer for 20 minutes, or until the custards are set, then remove the dishes and take off the foil. (The time it takes for the custards to set will depend upon how fast the water simmers – about 20 minutes should be right, but check them after 15 minutes.) Allow to cool, then chill overnight or for several hours. Turn out and serve with a jug of single cream. SERVES 4

# Apricot-stuffed Apples

*This is another recipe which would normally require oven cooking, but with a wok the dish can stand on the steaming rack and the fruit can be cooked quite successfully. Serve whipped cream or ice cream with the apples.*

225 g/8 oz dried apricots
grated rind and juice of 1 orange
4 tablespoons demerara sugar

4 large cooking apples
25 g/1 oz butter
25 g/1 oz flaked almonds

Roughly chop the apricots, then mix them with the orange rind and juice and the sugar. Core the apples and cut a horizontal slit round the outside of each apple to prevent it from bursting during cooking. Place the apples in a heatproof dish and spoon the apricot mixture into the centre of each. Cover the dish with foil, pinching the edge in just below the rim of the dish to prevent steam from entering during cooking, then stand the dish on the steaming rack in the wok.

Pour in enough water to come up to the level of the rack and bring the water to the boil, then put the lid on the wok and reduce the heat so that the water simmers steadily. Cook for 1 hour, checking to make sure that the water does not boil dry during cooking and adding more boiling water if necessary.

When the apples are cooked, pour the water out of the wok and wipe it out, then melt the butter in it and add the almonds. Fry the nuts until they are lightly browned, then sprinkle them over the fruit and serve immediately. SERVES 4

# Chinese-style Fruit Fritters

*Crisp, batter-coated pieces of apple and banana, coated with caramel and sprinkled with roasted sesame seeds, are mouth-watering. Remember that they are also quite filling so, if you're planning to serve them for dessert, make a light main course.*

2 bananas
2 cooking apples
100 g/4 oz self-raising flour
150 ml/$\frac{1}{4}$ pint water
2 eggs, separated
900 ml/1$\frac{1}{2}$ pints oil for deep frying

2 tablespoons roasted sesame
seeds
CARAMEL
100 g/4 oz sugar
100 ml/4 fl oz water

Cut the bananas into chunks. Peel, core and quarter the apples, then cut them into chunks.

Sift the flour into a mixing bowl and make a well in the centre. Pour in the water and add the egg yolks, then beat in the flour to make a smooth batter. Whisk the egg whites until very stiff, then fold them into the batter.

Pour the oil for deep frying into the wok and heat it to 190 C/375 F. Dip the pieces of fruit, a few at a time, into the batter and then cook them in the hot oil until crisp and golden. Remove with a slotted spoon and drain on absorbent kitchen paper. When you are about three-quarters of the way through cooking the fritters, place the sugar for the caramel in a saucepan with the water and bring to the boil, stirring occasionally until the sugar dissolves. Boil the sugar syrup hard until it reaches a light caramel – do not stir it at all once it starts boiling.

By now you should have finished cooking all the fritters and they should be draining on absorbent kitchen paper. Place them slightly apart on a large, lightly oiled platter and drizzle the caramel over them, turning them over with a fork to coat the other side in a little caramel. Sprinkle with the sesame seeds and serve immediately. SERVES 4

# Coconut-coated Bananas

*The coconut and egg white form a crisp coating on the bananas in this recipe and they are mouth-watering when served with clotted cream.*

8 small bananas
1 egg white
75 g/3 oz desiccated coconut
butter for frying

grated rind and juice of 2 oranges
4 tablespoons rum
3 tablespoons brown sugar

Dip the bananas in the egg white and coat them thoroughly in the coconut. Make sure that they are completely covered, adding a little more coconut and pressing it on well if necessary. Set to one side to allow the coating to harden slightly.

Melt a little butter in the wok and add the bananas, then fry until golden on the underside. Turn the bananas carefully to avoid breaking off the coconut, then cook until golden on the second side. Remove from the wok and arrange the bananas on a heated serving dish.

Add the remaining ingredients to the butter remaining in the wok and bring to the boil. Boil for a minute, then pour over the bananas and serve immediately. SERVES 4

# Pear and Plum Compote

*Illustrated on page 159*

*Served with clotted or whipped cream this fruit dessert is quite luscious.*

4 large ripe pears
450 g/1 lb plums
300 ml/½ pint rosé wine

100 g/4 oz sugar
grated rind of 1 small orange

Peel, quarter and core the pears, then place the fruit in the wok. Halve and stone the plums and add them to the pears. Pour in the wine, then stir in the sugar and orange rind.

Bring to the boil, then reduce the heat so that the syrup simmers gently and cook for 10 minutes. Serve immediately, or chill thoroughly and serve cold. SERVES 4

# Index